The Peach Who Thought She Had to Be a Coconut

Profound Reflections on the Power of Thought and Innate Resilience

Terry Rubenstein

With Brian Rubenstein

Illustrations by John Scott

This first edition published in 2017 by
Innate Health
66 Brent Street
London, NW4 2ES
www.innatehealth.co

Typography and layout by
Andrews UK Limited
www.andrewsuk.com

Cover designed by Dan Matalon

All proceeds from the sale of this book go toward supporting the non-profit educational programmes of Innate Health, registered charity number 1173025

Innate Health
Uncovering Resilience

Contents

Contents (cont.)

Foreword

Keith Blevens, Ph.D.

&

Valda Monroe

The book you are about to read is a collection of beautiful reflective essays by Terry Rubenstein. In every one, Terry demonstrates how the most important questions regarding resilience have been changed. What is the significance of this change and how did it begin?

In 1973, Sydney Banks, a ninth-grade-educated immigrant welder, "uncovered" (*not* discovered – a distinction he always insisted upon) the pre-existing psycho-logic paradigm of the Three Principles of Mind, Consciousness and Thought. Before this, we did not have a paradigm that explained both the apparent comings and goings of resilience. These Principles unified us all with both because they are the first elementary laws of the nature of mental life. They changed the questions of resilience forever.

Why? Because with them we uncover a deeper foundation and organisation to mental life. The deeper question now becomes, "How does our experience work psychologically?" In the absence of the Three Principles Paradigm, we had been less able to think specifically and deeply about *how* we psychologically experience life and, subsequently, how do we *not* psychologically experience life.

Because of this uncovering, we now know the single, definitive logic explaining where all feelings derive and how thought is catalysed into the reality we each now see. These Three Principles change resilience because they bring into clear focus the one hundred percent actual black-and-white logic humans have always been functioning according to. And, equally as important, they simultaneously invalidate the many false "paradigms" or "illogic" we all are *not* functioning according to. As we write this, can any of us really imagine how important, how powerful, this uncovering really is?

William James, the man known as the "father of American psychology", knew. He envisaged that such Principles would be more important to humankind than any technological development since fire. Why again? Because James knew that such elementary laws would create a necessary evolution in the mental resilience of the world.

When we had the opportunity to tell Sydney Banks about William James' prediction, Banks said James was remarkable because he had the honesty to say he did not know the answer to the "Principles of psychology" question. James knew psychology was a natural science. But because it yet had no laws, no Principles, it was in a pre-paradigm stage of development – like physics *before* Galileo. In 1890, he wrote that in psychology "...not the first glimpse of clear insight exists...we don't even know the terms between which the elementary laws would obtain if we had them. This is no science; it is only the hope of science."

As Professor Sonu Shamdasani, an eminent medical scholar and author, put it more recently, "One might do well to ask whether there could be a better description of the state of psychology today."

But an understanding of psychology without Principles is no more. A clear, immutable and universal logic that explains all psychological functioning has been revealed. We have entered a new era of understanding.

Sydney Banks was once famously asked by a person in his small town, "When did the true psychology begin?" His reply: "It began before the beginning of time." This answer was shocking. To us, this statement alone stands as but one testament of a paradigm breakthrough that civilisation must now take up and study.

So now, given all this, we can ask different questions and get different answers as to why have people been resilient throughout recorded history? We know now it is not because of such factors as the past, or upbringing, or the maximisation of protective factors, the minimisation of risk factors, or even vaguer answers such as faith or the indomitability of the human spirit. Nor can resilience any more be explained away as a deluxe cocktail combination of such factors. These are questions unwittingly limited by a "mixed" psychological paradigm we now know does not exist.

We live within this world of logic already, the actual paradigm of existence. We had clearly not known this truth, and what it renders obsolete, before. As Terry established in quoting Sydney Banks in her first book, *Exquisite Mind*:

"When psychologists stopped investigating the connection between mind and soul, they lost two of the most important clues to what they sought. They focused instead on behaviour, leading us away from our true psychological nature, ultimately encouraging us as passive victims of life."

We have always been resilient and always will be. Why? Because of how actual reality is being created. This is what William James predicted, what Sydney Banks realised, and what the logic of the Three Principles Paradigm establishes for the future of us all.

We are honoured to be a part of turning this page on human history and on our mutual misunderstandings about resilience.

Keith Blevens, Ph.D. and Valda Monroe,
La Conner, Washington,
April, 2017

Notes to Reader

A brief guide to getting the most out of these reflections

⚘ Each reflective piece finishes with a brief summary that I have called *"Blogsight"* – the key insight underpinning each blog. While of course no substitute for more in-depth understanding, I hope this will serve as a useful guide for your own journey of insightful learning.

⚘ Additionally, you will find selected key passages highlighted in bold where I have stepped outside of the narrative flow in order to emphasise a salient learning point that has more universal application.

⚘ I have made numerous references to *"our psychological experience"* of life. In my understanding there is no separation between the psychological and spiritual. One encompasses the other; one cannot exist without the other. They are two sides of the same coin. So I highly encourage you to read the word "psychological" with this in mind.

⚘ I use the terms *"logic"* and *"logical"* repeatedly. Logic is often associated with something solely of an intellectual nature. In my opinion, this is very limited. To me, logic is the deep spiritual order or pattern behind life. Logic reveals truth and therefore cannot be a human construct. Throughout the pages of this book, there is a fundamental, immutable logic that shatters the illusion of how we presume our reality is constructed and provides a clear direction for a new order of knowledge. This is the "logic" I am referring to. To limit this logic to the realm of the intellect is to do it a great disservice.

❀ Keith Blevens, my mentor and the co-author of this book's Foreword, in reference to the Three Principles, explains that the "wholeness and neutrality of all Mind, all Consciousness, all Thought cannot be separated nor can any one of them be split. They are each all true, all whole, at once." In my previous book, *Exquisite Mind*, I spoke of the Three Principles at length and defined each of them separately. In my current understanding, I often speak of them together. Sydney Banks, who uncovered and first articulated these Principles, said: "You must see in the singular if you want to find truth." Therefore any reference to "Thought in the moment" is a singular reference to Mind, Thought and Consciousness. They cannot exist independently. (I highly recommend you refer to the *Glossary and Definitions* at the end of the book for a better explanation of these and other key terms.)

❀ While the reflections tend to explore different subjects and experiences, you will find that the underlying key learning points are the same throughout the book. Essentially, I am saying the same salient ideas many times over, while doing so in a variety of ways. This is intentional. Truth is narrow but deep.

❀ Finally, you will undoubtedly notice that I frequently refer to "God" and the "divine". (Did I mention frequently?) For me, the single discriminator of "where do our feelings come from?" is the most direct route back to the singular truth of these spiritual Principles that are creating our reality, a direct route to source – or God. You may prefer other words such as "pre-existing intelligence", "Universal Mind" or something else that resonates for you. I am comfortable with the term "God" and do not intend it as a religious reference – at least not in this book. The logic of the inside-out paradigm points me back to God. If you don't like that word, feel free to change it in your own mind as you read along.

To our dear Innate Health colleagues, a wonderful team passionately committed to sharing truth and understanding

REFLECTIONS ON THE POWER OF THOUGHT AND INNATE RESILIENCE

The Peach Who Thought She Had to Be a Coconut

From a young age, I always believed that something about me did not feel quite right. It was a bit like when you venture out to work in the morning with your slippers on. You sense you are ill-equipped to deal with the day. Something has been overlooked. Something that is essential is missing. You just haven't looked down yet to figure out what.

This feeling took on many forms of insecure behaviour during my childhood and throughout my years of teenage angst. It rolled on into my twenties, gathering an ever-increasing, often ominous momentum. This feeling held within it a misunderstanding that was invisible to me for many years. And so I lived blindly within its apparent reality. This so-called truth – or more accurately, mistruth – had huge implications for my life.

At my core, I felt like a squidgy peach. The constitution of a peach was not what I desired or aspired to have. After all, who would want to be so unreliable? Juicy on a good day; overly soft and squelchy on a bad one. Who would choose to be intrinsically vulnerable, seemingly easy to be damaged and discarded? (And I knew all about the squelchy, squidgy nature of this erratic fruit – it was always the poor peaches my mother packed into the bottom of my lunch bag that were inevitably deposited mushed and squished in the school dustbin!)

Meanwhile, there was another fruit that held far greater appeal. The powerful coconut. This consistently strong, exotic, robust fruit (or nut, depending on your botanical bias) could be stepped on, dropped, thrown against a wall in frustration, used as a cricket ball, or even – in extreme circumstances – as a weapon. The coconut seemed to make it through all these ordeals, unscarred and intact; still round, still whole, still edible. I wanted to be a coconut.

So I had a problem. I felt like a peach. And aspired to be a coconut. Unsurprisingly, I concluded I was under-resourced and ill-equipped for life. I was thus doomed to feel self-conscious, anxious, exposed and hyper-sensitive to its outside variables. My mind was full of long, dark, cold winter days. And peaches don't fare well in the winter. So it made sense that I did not fare well in the winter of my mind. It felt like an unstoppable blizzard was constantly blowing through me. How could a soft, vulnerable peach survive such conditions?

Living with my assumptions about what a peach needed in order to survive and thrive, my skin felt sensitive to others' behaviours, my heart felt exposed to the threat of failure and rejection, and my soul felt vulnerable to life's predictably unpredictable ups and downs.

And so, in an effort to protect myself, I developed a number of strategies.

I worked hard and tried harder. Perhaps diligence and conscientious effort would toughen me up?

I binged and starved. Perhaps that would control the elements and drive away the demons?

I self-harmed and obsessively dreamed of escaping the persistently harsh environment not suited to a peach's fragile and sensitive outer layer. Perhaps that would bring me some relief?

I medicated and "sterilised" my mind. Perhaps I could simply disappear from the branches of my world, at least for a while?

I withdrew and tried to shelter behind other, more robust fruits – my husband and children – who appeared to be far more coconut than peach-like. Perhaps they could keep me safe?

And then, one day, as poignantly expressed by Albert Camus, "In the midst of winter, I found within me an invincible summer."

This stunned me. I was completely floored.

I realised I did not need to be a coconut. I had uncovered innate resilience. Innate health. It was – it is – my birthright. It is the birthright of humanity. A universal constant.

And then I realised something else. The coconut and me? We were not that different after all.

Resilience exists for all human beings. But we innocently erect false barriers that temporarily create the illusion that we are not resilient. The illusion that we are lacking and under resourced, that we are at the effect of the outside world, that we are ill-equipped to handle the vicissitudes of life.

2

I, like you, have weathered many storms in my lifetime. But facing life with this knowledge allows us to settle into our peachy skin knowing that we cannot be psychologically squished. We are as protected as the coconut. The squidgy peach is also a resilient peach.

For weeks, my writing team and I have grappled with the "right" title for this book. A great many suggestions were raised, considered, almost agreed upon – and then summarily discarded! Until yesterday. When reviewing the entire manuscript for a final time, one of the brilliant drawings of John Scott, the immensely talented illustrator of this book, stood out like a beacon. John had come up with a charming, deeply insightful sketch that perfectly captured the key message of the innate resilience that exists in the universe, the salient theme that lies at the heart of all of this book's reflections. John entitled this illustration, "The peach who thought she had to be a coconut."

And so, the inspiration for this essay came to be. And the inspiration for a somewhat unusual (dare I say "peachy"?) book title was born.

The peach and the coconut have far more in common than I once believed. Whatever the composition of their external skin, they can both feel vulnerable whenever they forget their true nature. And they can also both feel comfortable in their own skins each time they remember who they are at their core. They have both been ingeniously designed to be in the world.

All of the reflective essays that follow aim to explore and reveal the logic and truth behind this knowledge – the knowledge of the exquisite intricacy and flawlessness of our divinely created composition that eliminates the false assumption that we are non-resilient. This knowledge is self-evident once realised. And it carries with it a monumental implication, which I will phrase, believe it or not, as one of the most important questions a human being can ever ask:

Why would a peach ever want to be a coconut?

> BLOGSIGHT: *We have been perfectly designed for this world. This is what innate resilience is. It is the genius inherent in the fundamental composition of all human beings; of how we work psychologically and how we don't. Once realised, this knowledge will become more and more self-evident.*

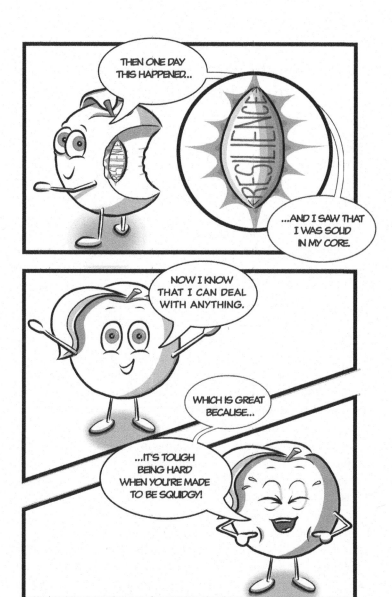

Thought as a Constant – Some Things Just Don't Change

For most of the first three decades of my life, there was one factor that destabilised me more than any other: the experience of feelings I did not like. I may have pointed a finger at situations (immigration, too many screaming babies, etc.), people (my easy-to-target, poor husband, my parents, etc.) and of course, yours truly (also an easy target). But though I did not know it at the time, it was never *really* about those factors.

For when I learned twelve years ago that none of these factors were guilty, my life flipped 180 degrees. I came face to face with the power of Thought and its intimate, inescapable connection with feeling. And I discovered that circumstances, past events and other people had never created – and could never create – any feeling within me.

Thought is a constant and behind it is every feeling I have ever had. A constant doesn't come and go. It is always there.

Has always been. And will always be.

A constant is reliable, predictable and of a deeper nature, which explains why scientists are always looking for constants. Because seeing how something works as a scientific fact or truth has monumental implications. Throughout history, when humans have stumbled upon pre-existing orders, their superstitions, self-made philosophies, beliefs, theories and assumptions were instantly dissolved. Personal truths instantly replaced with a universal truth.

Consider the discovery of a round earth, the revelation of a sun-centred solar system, or the unearthing of germs and their effect on human life. Before we knew that these truths had always been true, we were essentially making up the way things worked without knowing how right – or how wrong! – we were. Once these universal truths were uncovered, there came into place new logic that had huge implications that changed the world and the way we perceived it.

So here is another universal truth: we are always experiencing the power of *Thought in the moment.*

People often don't like change. Well, here is something that doesn't change, ever: the power of Thought creating your very own, perceived experience of life. From birth to death, you can only experience life through the power of Thought.

So how does this one irrefutable fact help us have a better life and make a better world?

The power of Thought creates our current impressions of the past (through memory), of the present (via attitudes, perceptions, feelings, moods, ideas, opinions) and of the future (by imagining, worrying, planning). Crucially, all thinking can only happen in the present moment. There is no other place we can experience thinking creating feeling.

Each time we realise that there is only one place our feelings come from – *Thought in the present moment* – we settle into a deeper truth that is revealed to us from within. This is an implication of seeing how it works. Having a singular cause always simplifies the equation. For example, once we realised that germs created childbed fever, our minds no longer had to consider all the other factors that we thought were the culprits, such as fear, curdled milk and hospital atmosphere.

When you do *not* see Thought as the singular, stand-alone cause of whatever you are experiencing, the implications of this misunderstanding will be that you will have multiple concerns to think about, figure out, chew on and worry about.

So the one essential discriminator or question is this: "Where do our feelings come from?"

And there is only one answer.

Our feelings are always coming from Thought in the moment. Never from anywhere else. Ever.

This deeper truth is the bedrock of our psychological experience. It is a constant. Whenever we feel a need to drop thinking, control thinking, find a better thought, uncover wisdom, arrive at clarity, not take our thinking too seriously, or do anything else to Thought, we are forgetting where our experience comes from. To realise that it comes from the infinite power of the Mind in each moment is to reconnect with what is true.

Truth makes no judgement of us. We may judge how we are feeling. Others may judge us for how we are feeling. But the truth is the truth. It doesn't judge. It just is.

Thought is of a pure, divine nature. It cannot change its nature. You can misunderstand and forget that what you are feeling is Thought. But Thought is still Thought. Neither good nor bad. Just Thought. A constant.

When we forget this, we try and control, change, seek, wait or let go. This will always be the case. Just like when we forget that the earth moves, so we speak about the sun rising and setting. It looks this way to us. But it is, as even my five-year-old son knows, a fundamental error. The sun never moves.

There exists a state of deep psychological rest that needs no changing or doing when our understanding is aligned with the truth that we are always and only ever experiencing the power of Thought. Inherent in this truth is no separation between clarity and contamination, wisdom and irrationality, positivity or negativity.

The world in which we live seems to be changing fast. Our personal life circumstances and our relationships also seem to be in a state of constant flux. However, the fact that you will only ever know your circumstances, your life, your job, your loved ones, yourself, your worst nightmare and your best daydream via your thinking in the moment, will never change. This completely reliable fact is what is sometimes called "innate health".

Innate health is to discover a centre of gravity that will never move or change. Experiencing this truth *is* resilience and psychological stability.

(Don't confuse this with feeling good or calm, which is far less appealing than your connection to that which is divine and constant.)

8

Our innate health is our psychological and spiritual life force. Pull the plug and we would cease to know we are alive. It is the source of yet-to-be-discovered knowledge, love, compassion, peace. It has told a thousand tales of resilience and has all these gifts nesting in its bosom.

The challenge is to see that this bedrock is what lies behind all the change we feel. That there is no other factor, force, law, person, event or circumstance that has had, or will have, the power to make us feel or experience anything – other than the power of Thought. How simple. Only one single thing.

You can't get away from it. There are no exceptions. It's one hundred percent. A fact.

A constant.

BLOGSIGHT: *The one essential discriminator or question is this: "Where do our feelings come from?" And there is only one answer: our feelings are always coming from Thought in the moment. Never from anywhere else.*

All Excuses off the Table – The Genesis of the Three Principles

*T*he *Genesis of the Three Principles* is a recently made documentary that tells the story of Sydney Banks' experience when he had his original, incredibly enlightening insight into the nature of the Mind over four decades ago. It is a powerful, moving and fascinating account of the profound clarity and pure understanding that Syd (as he is affectionately known) arrived at. One of the core themes stressed by the filmmakers Elsie Spittle and Chip Chipman, dear friends of Syd and amongst the first generation teachers of these Principles, is the importance of appreciating where this understanding came from.[1]

I completely agree. Twelve years ago, I was gifted to have my own "mini-enlightenment experience". Trust me, I did not wake up to the oneness of life or see into the depth of Thought as Syd did – I am still waiting for that one! However, in my own small way, I fell out of a great deal of misunderstanding so that life looked far simpler, far more hopeful and far more beautiful.

It was not what I expected to find. But was I ever happy that I did!

It gifted me the certainty and confidence to know that my potential to live a wonderful life was far greater than I had ever imagined. At the same time, I realised that this was a "human thing" *not* a "Terry thing". In other words, whether we know it or not, we *all* have a nature that is

---

[1] Sydney Banks, a Scottish-born welder living on the north-west coast of North America, had a profound experience in 1973 in which he generated deep insight into the workings of the human psyche. Over time, he articulated this insight as fundamental principles that explained the entire human psychological experience. These became known as the Three Principles of Mind, Consciousness and Thought. (Also known as the Principles of Innate Health or Health Realisation. These terms will be capitalised to indicate they are referring to Principles in this book.) Sydney Banks soon began sharing his insights, revealing a profound logic on which a new understanding of mental, emotional and spiritual well-being for all people was based.

divinely inspired. We then get to have a psychological experience of life via the gift of Thought – which I like to call God's "fairy-dust" – and so we create our own version of reality every moment that we are alive.

When I realised this, I also realised that I had everything I needed for the rest of my life. I was done. My suitcase was fully packed. For all seasons. There was nothing intrinsic within me that was lacking or missing. For the first time I felt ready and able to face the rest of my life, with all the challenges and all the living that was still to come.

The reason I fell in love with the Principles of Mind, Consciousness and Thought was not just because they were true and logical, not just because they are an explanation that unifies all psychological life, and not just because they are so helpful, practical and at the same time, of the deepest spiritual nature. Though of course all of those reasons would have been more than sufficient to justify my passion and excitement. I fell in love with this learning because it showed me how we are all operating out of a level playing field. It takes every excuse known to human beings off the table and says: "If you are human, you are bound by the truth of these gifts. You cannot work outside of them. And if you are human, you are elevated by these gifts. They are your nature and are perfectly divine."

A level playing field? Every excuse (and I have heard some pretty compelling ones) off the table? Really?

Well, once you know who Sydney Banks was and what he did (or more pertinently, did *not* do) prior to making this discovery, then it all makes sense. Syd was not an educated professional; he was not schooled in matters of the psyche and the soul; he was not even overtly searching for answers. He had grown up with challenging circumstances, and on the face of it, he actually had nothing in his arsenal to suggest that he would be a good candidate for this experience. I mean, who would have thought that a middle-aged man with a lilting Scottish accent would be *the* person to see right through the illusion that mistakenly assumes that our feelings are coming from something other than Thought in the moment? Who would have thought that someone working in a mill as a welder would uncover the fundamental truth of how life works?

One could argue that even little old me might have been better equipped to make this discovery. At least I was kind of desperate and obviously looking for something. And I was pretty well read, if I say so myself. (Self-help and Mind, Body, Spirit books were my thing after all!) So if there had been any kind of democratic vote for candidates to uncover the Principles, I – and no doubt many others who were seeking and searching – may have had the edge over Syd.

But the fact that it was Sydney Banks – warts and all – *is* the point.

For it shows that the Principles are unconditional. Their perfect, pre-existing logic is alive and operating within us all no matter who we are or what our backgrounds or foregrounds are. Mind needs no form or conditions within which to operate. Just a soul to reveal itself to.

Syd shared an exquisite gift with the world. I was privileged to get to know him a little towards the end of his life. And from my brief personal interactions and the many stories I heard about him, he had no intention of being a guru to anyone or an expert on how our minds work.

He, more than any of us, understood that true knowledge does not belong to any one person. It belongs to everyone. He knew true knowledge was not something he could give away. It is within every person's consciousness already and was not his to give. It was and is God's gift to us all.

To appreciate the genesis of this understanding is to know that these Principles are always alive within you. They connect you to your spiritual essence while at the same time allowing you to be extraordinarily human. Sydney Banks showed us that what he found is within us too. It is our nature, our heritage.

And it just happens to be the explanation of how the entire human experience works.

BLOGSIGHT: *The Principles are unconditional. Their perfect, pre-existing logic is alive and operating within us all no matter who we are or what our backgrounds or foregrounds are. Mind needs no form or conditions within which to operate.*

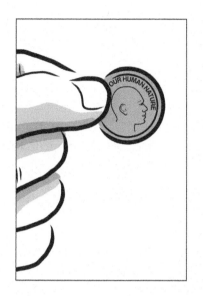

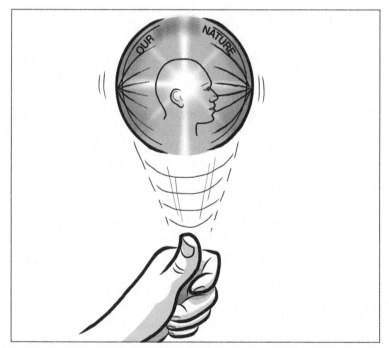

Is Thought Bad?

This week I was reflecting on our recently submitted application for the Innate Health Centre to become an independent, officially registered charity in the UK.

The idea of an Innate Health Centre was borne of a thought. All ideas are.

I clearly remember the day, almost four years ago, when I was out running with my husband and that first thought of opening a centre popped into my mind. I even recall the exact moment and place – and the wonderful rush of inspiration that accompanied it. We had just exited Hampstead Heath via Kenwood House and were running down the hill that is Winnington Road. (This road is always the subject of a vigorous debate between Brian and I; my husband is convinced it is a sharp and arduous incline when running up it, while I am of the correct opinion that it is nothing more than a gentle slope. Talk about separate realities!)

But here's what's interesting. Today, the Innate Health Centre seems like such an obvious fact: a busy organisation committed to educating people, especially young people, about the inside-out logic of the mind and our innate resilience. However, before the *thought* of it occurred, the centre did not exist in either space or time. Neither did it exist in my or anyone else's consciousness. When it arrived as a thought, it then became rooted in the reality of the universe so that it could be nurtured and developed.

It's fascinating to recall how, at the time of my initial inspiration, I had absolutely no idea of what a centre for mental and emotional well-being looked like. I hadn't come across one before. (Shopping centres, yes, but Innate Health centres – no!) Other than a deep intuition that this was the right direction to pursue, I just followed my nose – moment by moment, thought after thought – until the clarity of this vision swam into focus. Each piece of the puzzle slowly emerged, in its own time. I remember walking around our offices holding a large piece of white, torn off flip-chart paper with the word "centre" scribbled in the middle, going from person to person asking for their input regarding this embryonic idea. Bit by bit, our thinking converged and created the model that in time became the Innate Health Centre.

This organic process of creation, direction and vision for the Centre still remains: being responsive to inspiration and opportunities as they show up, and enjoy the falling away of already-formed ideas or programmes when they either do not make sense anymore or are replaced by current or more relevant ones. And here's what stands out for me when I reflect on that process.

Everything comes from somewhere. Everything always derives from Thought – the universal spiritual or unformed energy from which all form derives. This is true of both physical form (nature, as we sometimes call it) and non-physical form (concepts, ideas, inspiration, opinions, attitudes and feelings).

This process of giving birth to the Centre didn't always feel like it was initiated through Thought. We just lived it and made it happen. But as is always the case, its origins lay in the energy of Thought. Each step of the way we added and subtracted, adjusted and adapted to the vision first formed on that decline down Winnington Road. We have done this only through the power of Thought. We couldn't have done it any other way. It is the *only* way.

The creative process is a constant. It is an in-the-moment mechanism always in motion for all of us and for all of life. It enables us to adjust, see afresh and move forward. Put simply, it allows us to think, think some more, and think again.

All of this got me wondering why Thought is often given such a bad rap. Many current psychologies speak of our thoughts as the "bad guys", the troublemakers who need to be put in their place, silenced, controlled, changed, redirected, reframed or – if we are feeling particularly compassionate – ignored completely. It's like putting a misbehaving child on the naughty step!

When Sydney Banks had his deep insight into the nature of the Mind, he immediately articulated that insight with these pithy words:

"All insecurity comes from Thought."

Here are a few other insights that Sydney Banks shared about this incredible capacity we call Thought:

Thought is a divine gift.

Thought is the creative agent we use to direct us through life.

Thought is a completely neutral gift... But it is what we, as humans, put into our thoughts that dictate what we think of life.

Those who had the opportunity to listen and learn from Syd heard something in his tone and feeling that went beyond his actual words. When Syd spoke about Thought, it was with an undeniable awe and respect in his voice. It did not sound as if he was speaking about an insidious and dangerous enemy from which we needed to protect ourselves, or to take up arms against. To my mind, he was describing an energy that was pure, creative and benevolent. And way beyond anything we mortals can mess with anyhow.

A simple analogy: We all breathe. But does it ever occur to any of us to give that fact a hard time, a bad reputation? Probably not, even though there are moments when we may be out of breath, gasping for breath, breathing too heavily or over-conscious of our breathing – or someone else's for that matter? (How about the guy sitting next to you on a small plane coming back from Oslo?)

We understand that to breathe is to live. It is a vital and essential inbuilt part of our physiology. Breathing doesn't require anything from us: it regulates itself and does its job as it was perfectly designed to do so.

Thought is akin to the psychological breath of life. Everything we experience is created from Thought. Every idea, every object, every relationship, every conflict, every concept... As my friend and colleague, Mara Gleason, aptly expresses it: "There is nothing we see in this world that was not created or borne out of Thought."

Thought is a divine gift. Yes, of course we have free will, which allows us to bring this gift into our lives in many different ways. But we cannot change, reframe or manipulate the raw materials of something that is divinely inspired. No scientist has ever considered recreating the breath.

When we stop being afraid of our thinking – which also means not being afraid of our feelings as they are *always* interconnected – and we lay down our arms and weapons, something extraordinary begins to happen. We begin to learn something deeper about Thought, about how it does and does not work.

And learning about Thought is to learn about all three Principles of Mind, Consciousness and Thought, for they play together as rhythmically and seamlessly as the harmonious sounds of the perfect orchestra. They play no other way. Whatever music you listen to via their sounds is always an expression of the divine tune of the universe.

And if they are not playing a tune that you enjoy listening to, perhaps you need to step back and consider why. For how is it even possible that the instruments of the divine can ever sound anything but flawlessly perfect?

BLOGSIGHT: *Thought is the psychological breath of life; everything we experience is created from the power of Thought. While free will allows us to bring this gift into our lives in many different ways, we cannot change, reframe or manipulate the raw materials of something that is divinely inspired.*

There Is Mental Health in Mental Life

I recently spent a number of hours online reading about the life and work of William James. James, who died in 1910, is recognised by many as the "Father of American Psychology" and was one of the very early presidents of the American Psychological Association. He was a philosopher, physician and the first educator to offer a psychology course in the United States. (Thank you, Wikipedia!)

It was very reaffirming to discover that a pioneer and luminary in the field of psychology and philosophy understood something so crucial about the human condition. James grasped that mental health is not a hit-or-miss phenomena, a realm belonging to only certain individuals while remaining out of bounds for many others.

Mental health is not random. It is not the domain of the privileged or the educated or those who win the genetic or biochemical lottery.

James believed it was coded into the blueprint of our spiritual and psychological DNA. However, he knew that the field had yet to uncover and articulate the principles that would reveal this health, as a constant and as a science.

William James had his own mental health struggles. My online research revealed that for almost three years after receiving his MD, James lived in his family home battling ill health and depression. He would later describe this depression as a "crisis of meaning" brought on by his studies in science. This depression left him feeling that there was no ultimate meaning in life and that his belief in free will and God were illusions. James suffered panic attacks and hallucinations just like his father before him, which caused him to believe that his illness was rooted in a biological determinism he could not overcome.

One day when he was in his late twenties, after reading an essay by the 19th century French philosopher, Charles Renouvier, James' psychological fever began to subside. He came to believe that free will was not an illusion. As he writes in his journal from that time:

> *I think that yesterday was a crisis in my life. I finished the first part of Renouvier's second essay and see no reason why his definition of free will – "the sustaining of a thought because I choose to when I might have other thoughts" – need be the definition of an illusion. At any rate, I will assume for the present – until next year – that it is no illusion. My first act of free will shall be to believe in free will.*

James had an insight that collapsed his previous "depressed thinking". Consequently, as he expresses above so powerfully, his depression became yesterday's reality.

We have been privileged to live in a generation in which the fundamental principles of psychology have now been uncovered. Mind, Consciousness and Thought give us the blueprint that explains all human psychological functioning. They categorically assert that there is indeed mental health in mental life.

What was William James' dream is our reality – and always has been. This presents us with a responsibility to reawaken ourselves, our children and future generations to this reality. In a world that often seems so full of confusion, misunderstanding, suffering and despair, there is a light that illuminates the way for us all. It is the light of truth and pure logic. It is what we mean when we speak of innate health. It is the innate resilience with which we have all been blessed.

Let's continue to build on the foundation that William James began. A good place to begin is by understanding and appreciating that we have all been granted psychological health as a perfectly divine gift. Seeing that fact deeper and deeper within ourselves will give us the capacity to see it more and more in others.

And it gives us the hope that we can look forward to the time when it will be known and lived as a universal truth.

BLOGSIGHT: *Mental health exists in mental life. It is not random, belonging to certain individuals while remaining out of bounds for others. Knowing that it is available to us all brings great hope.*

What Is Innate Health and Does It Have Anything to Do with Feeling Good?

In the past, I thought that *innate health* or *resiliency* (two ways of expressing the same concept) was a personal or individual characteristic intrinsic to all human beings. This was only after I learned that it existed at all. Before that, it didn't even register as being relevant to me. In fact, the notion of innate health was as fantastical to me as fairies or garden gnomes (no offence intended to those who are believers!).

As I gradually learned more about the workings of the Mind, I have come to appreciate that what exists within me as a constant, must exist as a constant in the universe as well. The implication of this is that resiliency or mental health is part of *all* life – not just part of each one of us as individuals. By virtue of being alive, we are all blessed to be recipients of this offering. It is genetically encoded into the blueprint of the universe.

This week I read a powerful essay by Lord Jonathan Sacks – the previous Chief Rabbi of the United Kingdom, author of over thirty books and the recipient of the 2016 Templeton Prize – which beautifully expressed this idea. Lord Sacks writes that after a lecture he gave a number of years ago at Cambridge University, he was handed a book by Sir Martin Rees (now Baron Rees), President of the Royal Society, winner of the 2011 Templeton prize, and widely regarded as Britain's most distinguished scientist.

The book, *Just Six Numbers – the deep forces that shape the universe*, explains how the universe is shaped by six mathematical constants which, had they varied by a millionth or trillionth degree, would have resulted in no universe or at least no life. In Lord Sacks' words: "Had the force of gravity been slightly different, for example, the universe would have expanded or imploded in such a way as to preclude the formation of the stars and planets. Had nuclear efficiency been slightly lower the cosmos would consist only of hydrogen; no life would have emerged. Had it been slightly higher, there would have been rapid stellar evolution and decay, again leaving no time for life to emerge."

Lord Sacks proceeds to explain how, in the Bible, there is incredible attention given to the precise dimensions and workings regarding the construction of the Tabernacle (the portable structure that was a centre of worship for the Jewish people in the period after their exodus from Egypt). Lord Sacks further points out that the Tabernacle was a microcosm of the world God made. "It was meant to signal, powerfully and palpably, that God exists throughout the cosmos; a man-made structure to mirror and focus attention on the divinely-created universe." What existed in the Tabernacle existed in the world.

This brings me back to resilience or innate health. The "resilience coding" is inherent within me and it is also inherent within all individuals, families, schools, communities, institutions and governments. And, wait for it, this coding is also inherent within the world. What makes a resilient individual is the same coding that makes a resilient world. It is not personal. It is a constant.

The false barriers we erect that betray or make this coding feel like the property of the lucky few, will be the same barriers that schools, institutions, society and countries erect. Fear, confusion, anger, discord, conflict and insecurity are borne of the same fabric – whether you are little me or big old Russia. They are borne of Thought but are erroneously and dangerously attributed to outside factors. (For me, that appears in the form of the work-life balance and public speaking. For Russia, that most likely looks like Ukraine or the USA, though you would have to ask Russia to be sure as I am no expert on this topic.)

Innate health does not mean we feel good all the time. In fact, it has nothing to do with how we feel. It is not about a particular feeling. It is not contingent on feelings. Feelings come and go as our thinking changes. But how our system operates does not change. It is a constant – something that is always there.

Me and Thought, you and Thought, the world and Thought. Nothing else can squeeze in and affect us psychologically. This is a spiritual and scientific fact.

Like Sir Martin Rees discovered, the implications of this understanding is for the world, not just for us as individuals. This is a truth of a deeper nature than existing theories or philosophies about the mind. So these implications are enormous if seen. And potentially catastrophic if not.

But there is always hope, because something that is constant works whether we are aware of it or not. No person is excluded from the blessings of that which is constant. Ultimately, all it takes is an opening of our hearts and minds to see what is already there.

BLOGSIGHT: *Innate health does not mean we feel good all the time. In fact, it has nothing to do with how we feel; it is not contingent on feelings. Feelings come and go as our thinking changes. But how we operate does not change.*

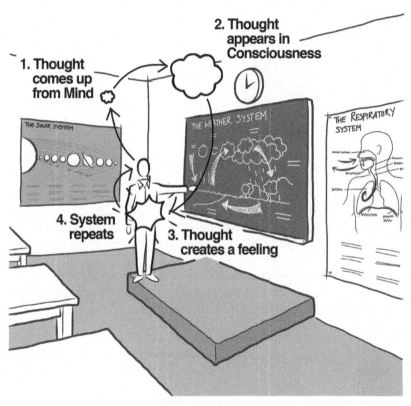

The Innate Health / Resiliency System

Why Our Fear of Feeling Bad Is
Creating More Psychological Distress

*If people would only learn not to be afraid of their own experience,
that alone would change the world.*

—Sydney Banks

Society holds a deep-rooted conviction that we need to be more aware of mental illness, lest it be swept under the carpet or stigmatised in any way. This approach may be informed by compassion and a worthy aspiration to alleviate suffering. But it is also based on an easy-to-miss, critical misunderstanding that is a huge pitfall for us. Consequently, without intending to, society is innocently contributing to the very problem it seeks to alleviate.

We need not be afraid of our own experience. **The implication of this statement is enormous and challenges one of the most fundamental psychological dogmas inherent in the world today.**

Society often reverts to extreme measures in an attempt to rectify a perceived oversight or "wrong". We overcorrect past mistakes like we overexert on the steering wheel when we feel the car skidding out of control. This is true of many of the current prevailing views regarding emotional and psychological distress.

For generations, it seems that many parents were not aware that their children had an emotional life (at least, that's what my parents told me!). Resources for understanding the human dimension field were limited; there were very few psychological or parenting books around at the time. The predominant attitude of many who grew up during or post-war was that people should "dig deep and get on with life no matter what". Yet I have often heard parents and grandparents lament about feelings of guilt and regret regarding how they understood, or more accurately, misunderstood the inner worlds of their children. They were not cognisant of their children's pain or sufficiently responsive to their emotional sensitivities. This omission carried significant consequences.

In response to this oversight, a new intense scrutiny emerged, characterised by iterative questions such as, "How are we are doing?" and "How are our kids doing?" The pendulum has swung violently in the other direction. Now, we all notice and deal with emotional upset. The overarching aim: to avoid any so-called "signs of psychological damage". Protecting children from psychological distress has become a number-one priority.

As someone who has devoted my professional life to working in the mental health field (and not to mention, mother of six children), I absolutely endorse the societal shift towards greater awareness and prioritisation of mental well-being, especially in young people. But this shift had also come at a great cost: fear of our emotional experience. And fear of our children's emotional experiences. Many of us, me included for the first thirty years of my life, have become paranoid when we seem not to be doing well or feel bad. Our tolerance for psychological discomfort and hardship has gone way down.

Meanwhile, we have made up for our previous "sins" (or those of our parents) by buying an army of parenting and self-help books, most of which imply something along the lines of, "If you are aware and careful enough, Johnny won't suffer." The emergence of a plethora of psychological theories, therapeutic approaches and personal development methods has bolstered our efforts. These conscientiously promote the core theme: we can stop you feeling bad and help you feel better if you talk through your problems enough or try these techniques.

An insidious message has seeped in, becoming deeply ingrained in our upbringing and our culture. If you feel anxious, down, insecure, stressed, disappointed, rejected or hurt – well, this could be the start of something really serious! Every time we begin to feel as if we are struggling, our internal alarm bells start ringing, as well as the bells of our loved ones. Uncomfortable feelings become intolerable. Refusing to address these feelings is labelled "denial" or "unhealthy". And not dealing with being upset by talking about or medicating it means you may never "get better". Despite the noble intent, this is a vicious circle, not a virtuous one.

So we have lost sight of our inherent capacity to get over emotional upset, even when those feelings are extreme. We have forgotten that there is nothing that needs to be healed. We have lost faith and confidence in our own innate, psychological immune system – commonly called resilience. We have naively bought into our own emotional vulnerabilities and fragility. We have forgotten that we were born whole, not broken.

And then we innocently pass this belief on to the next generation. "Don't worry if you are not feeling good, we will help put it right." We misguidedly give our children these messages:

"We will control your environment as best we can, to help you avoid feeling bad."

"We will sort out your school, social and academic life to protect you. Without this assistance, you cannot cope."

"We will send you for help so that you feel confident, happy and immune to emotional upset." (As if that is possible – to develop immunity from feeling bad!)

"We will get you the meds and therapy needed to take away the pain you are feeling."

I want to stress that there may be times for psychiatric medication, professional support and practical assistance. However, there is a prevailing belief that maintains that these approaches are ultimately *the* answers to psychological distress and to finding a healthy emotional equilibrium.

This is way off the mark. Yes, meds may be helpful, if not advisable at times. But far too often, this is a knee-jerk response to our own discomfort with feeling bad. We project this onto our children and the rest of society – and it quickly becomes a dangerous and slippery slope.

When we assume it is not OK to feel bad, or even feel *really* bad, we are missing the fact that we are connected to a Mind that is healthy and whole. Every second we are alive, this Mind via the power of Thought creates "in the moment" thinking that we experience and

feel. These sensory manifestations of Thought cannot damage us, no matter how extreme they feel nor what traumatic event they have been connected to. Although it often looks otherwise through the eyes of misunderstanding, these feelings cannot hurt us. There is no dent that requires repair.

This is so simple that it's overlooked. We are merely caught in the illusion of misunderstanding – of mistakenly assuming that our feelings are coming from something other than Thought in the moment.

But the logic doesn't work this way. Our feelings are only ever coming from our thinking. From the inside-out. Knowing this, we can settle into a deep, unshakeable confidence. The constant river of Thought means that whether we will it or not, new thinking will arise for us. New cells have new memories. New thoughts have new feelings. Insight is the antibiotic of the mind.

Due to our misunderstanding of where fear comes from, we overlook this self-evident truth. I continue to do so. But each time we remember, we can share it with our children so that they too can learn the folly of looking outside in order to fix what was created by their own minds in the first place. Emotional and psychological pain originates from the Mind; its resolution can therefore only come from the Mind. If we don't realise this, we will forever be selling ourselves and the next generation short.

A good measure for parents is: are we OK with our kids not being OK? Are we willing to give our children the message that it is OK to feel bad? That it is actually normal. That it is nothing to be afraid of. That it is part of the natural ebb and flow of their psychological system.

We are not being neglectful if we fail to panic when our loved ones are not doing well. It's OK to grieve and feel bereft. It's OK to wake up with a feeling of anxiety and dread. It's OK to be overwhelmed and stressed. It's OK to feel self-conscious and lacking in confidence. It's OK to be confused. And it's OK to feel really down.

Yes, there are times when we need support and there are different ways to get this. We have a creative and responsive mind to help us discern which support is necessary and when. Our common sense is designed to help us determine how to deal with our challenges as they emerge. But common sense operates best not when it is dictated to us by outside theories or fears, but rather from a secure and well-functioning mind that is in sync with a deeper order of reality.

To the extent that we have a correct understanding of where our feelings come from – the thinking we are having in that moment – we are more likely to be considered and thoughtful about how to deal with ourselves. Consequently, we will act responsibly and appropriately.

But if we have not yet learned about how the human experience works, we will reach outwards rather than inwards. And the results will be different. At worst, we will generate more of what we are trying to run away from. At best, we will stick on a plaster that will inevitably peel off a short while later. Unless we begin to educate ourselves and future generations about the origins of psychological distress and emotional upset, we will continue to further destabilise ourselves, our families and our society.

By overprotecting ourselves and our loved ones, we are insidiously cultivating a dangerous message: human beings are mentally fragile. We thereby smother the innate, natural resilience we were all born into.

Insightfully seeing this will take care of the so-called stigma.

In fact, it makes it a non-issue to begin with.

BLOGSIGHT: *When we assume it is not OK to feel uncomfortable, we are failing to recognise that our feelings are always coming from our thinking. This one error in logic compels us to attempt to avoid or change these feelings. But our innate resilience axiomatically implies that these sensory manifestations of Thought cannot damage or hurt us, no matter how extreme they feel.*

We Are All Equally Disabled – And Abled

My friend Brett Chitty was born profoundly deaf. Understandably, this physical disability challenged him immensely. Brett movingly describes living as a recluse for eight years, suffering throughout that time from severe depression. By his own admission, he spent years feeling extremely alienated from those he considered more "able" and less "disabled".

Last week I heard Brett speak of how, in the past, he was terrified every time he attended the all-too frequent hospital appointments that his hearing disability necessitated. These visits left him feeling disadvantaged, destabilised and vulnerable. Disabled.

Consequently, Brett always made sure his father accompanied him to these medical appointments, to be his ears and voice. While that seemed to work out practically, emotionally, it felt less than satisfying.

Brett speaks about the numerous powerful insights he generated from what he calls the *logic of the single paradigm.*

To put it simply, the mind works one way. We only ever experience our thinking in each moment. We only feel what we think. However, when we forget this crucial psychological fact, we innocently split Thought and feeling. When we fall into this illusion, we cannot help but assume that our feelings are coming from our circumstances or something other than Thought in the moment.

In Brett's case, he assumed that his feelings were a direct result of his lack of hearing and his inability to carry a coherent dialogue with the doctors. He was convinced that the entire hospital experience was responsible for his overwhelming feelings of fear and insecurity.

But that all changed when Brett arrived at a radically different understanding of the cause of his emotional "reactions". He describes an extremely powerful insight that occurred to him in the hospital when he suddenly realised he was making a huge mistake, illogically living as though there were objects outside of Thought that were creating his feeling. And as the misunderstanding fell away, he found himself conversing fluently with the doctors and consultants.

We have an intelligence that hears for us, sees for us, thinks for us and knows for us. As Brett says, "I have learnt that we don't hear with our ears. We hear through our thinking."

Upon learning this from Brett, I realised something I had often wondered about. How could Helen Keller (the famous early 20th century American author and political activist who was deaf, dumb and blind) learn to speak, when she could not see or hear? She had virtually no outside stimulus. She was essentially locked in. How was meaningful communication with other people remotely possible?

When we understand that we are seeing, hearing and experiencing the world of our minds, hearts and inner consciousness, Helen Keller's incredible story finally makes sense. This remarkable and inspirational woman learned to speak from Thought in the moment. From within her soul.

Once Thought and feeling are united, outside circumstances such as illness, "difficult" people, hospitals and so on, cannot ever create feelings within us.

As human beings, we will inevitably have many feelings about these and other events: sadness, fear, stress, calm, ambivalence, paralysis, anger or hopelessness, to name a few.

But whatever those feelings are, they will *always* be a manifestation of Thought.

When we fall asleep to this deeper truth, we feel like Brett – disabled. Not just physically, but psychologically as well. Sometimes we *are* temporarily disabled. But in truth, just like Brett found out, we are always equally able. It's a level playing field. The same rules apply for everyone.

Waking up to this deep spiritual logic brings us back into its bosom where we feel unified rather than isolated. Some people call this living in wisdom. Some call it going inside. Some call it living one's best self. Some call it resilience.

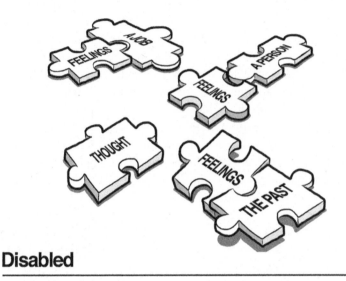

Disabled

Abled

Brett's story is our story. It is a story that has been around throughout history. Moses thought that his inability to articulate himself through speech would render him an ineffective leader. (The Bible conveys that Moses had some form of speech impediment.) In response to his concerns, God reassured him that his apparent speech limitation would be nothing of the sort. His so-called "disability" would turn out to be one of his greatest abilities – the vehicle through which Moses would educate, inspire, prophesise and lead.

Amazingly, Brett is now a speaker, mentor, website-creator and inspiration to many people who know him directly or have heard his story. His story is evidence to the powerful fact that as one becomes more psychologically unified, one discovers the capacity to actually do away with supposed disabilities.

Brett's story also helps wake us up to our own misunderstanding of where our limitations and barriers originate. He teaches us that each time we align ourselves with the wholeness of our moment-to-moment psychological experience, we get in touch with a deep spiritual intelligence that is "able" beyond our wildest dreams. And then we get to surprise ourselves by discovering that what we previously assumed to be impossible is actually very possible.

Spiritually and psychologically, the disabled becomes abled.

BLOGSIGHT: *When we innocently split Thought and feeling, we feel temporarily disabled. Once Thought and feeling are reunited, we realised we were always equally abled.*

What Are Your False Gods?

I recently had the special opportunity of co-facilitating a retreat in the idyllic setting of a country farmhouse in the Cotswolds. The participants were a wonderful and warm group of Orthodox Chassidic women: kind, generous, open-hearted and full of fantastic questions that sit at the heart of the inside-out logic of the workings of the Mind.

During the penultimate session, I said something new that just popped out of my mouth and instantly silenced the room – because of all things, it concerned idol worship! This is what I shared:

"When we objectify our feelings – another way of saying that we innocently but falsely believe our feelings are a result of some object other than Thought – we unintentionally create a form of idolatry. We are now engaged in idol worship."

These words not only shocked me, but the ladies listening as well. There was a collective intake of breath. The room fell very quiet. And then they asked me to say it again.

I was a bit surprised at myself. This was not an idea I had planned on expressing – I had actually never said such a thing before. But I felt its impact in my heart and I knew it was true for me. I also create and give power to objects and outside factors, innocently anointing and giving a god-like status to these factors in my mind. (Even the London weather has been given god-like status for crying out loud! I am for sure guilty of this one – especially in the seemingly never-ending dark, wet, days of late February!)

In these specific moments, I am innocently operating with a faulty logic. I worship false gods. I blame them for my distress or give them credit for my good fortune, like the many people who throughout time have blamed their multiple gods of choice for their suffering or happiness.

This may sound extreme. But in truth, in assuming that something other than Thought can be the cause of our feelings, I – we – indeed mistakenly appear to give power to something other than the one constant source of all experience. You can call it the Mind. You can call it the force or energy of God. You can call it a higher intelligence. You can call it the power of Thought.

When we split Thought and feeling and believe that something or somebody else has power over our psychological or feeling state, it is as if we are handing over God's power to other multiple gods (capital "G" and small "g" intentional), that do not actually exist. These gods can show up in our minds as people, illness, our boss, our family, our messy house, our critics and even our biggest fans – anyone or anything we attribute to the cause of our feeling state.

In one of my favourite books, *A Thousand Names for Joy*, Byron Katie recalls visiting a dear friend in hospital who was battling cancer. Byron Katie asked this friend, who was understandably fearful of her illness, "Do you love God?"

"Yes, of course!" her friend replied.

Byron Katie then uttered these extraordinary words: "You can't love God if you don't love cancer."

While challenging to hear, it is very enlightening if we push ourselves a little further. Fear – that powerful emotion that we all know well – can only ever come from Thought. And the origin of all Thought is Mind, God-Mind. There is only one source for our all of our felt experience of life, including the fear of a terminal illness.

This, I believe, was Byron Katie's loving message to her friend. You cannot split Thought and feeling. And if you understand the nature and origin of Thought, you will understand the nature and origin of all emotions – even the fear of cancer. But in believing that our experience of this illness is separate from Thought, we attribute to it a power that it simply cannot have. We innocently turn cancer into a false god.

Cancer is something way beyond my experience, but my friend Wendy Saggese inspires me with her relationship to her Stage 4 cancer diagnosis. I am sure she has had many fearful and vulnerable moments, but she has also had deep insight into the powerlessness that cancer has to make her feel any particular way. There was a time when this illness was a dominant presence in Wendy's past, when she assumed it was the protagonist of the shadows of her fear. But Wendy now lives more awake to the understanding that cancer has no power to cast such shadows. The shadows, Wendy explains, are made up of Thought. The cancer is the illness she has. The circumstance. She will have many different shadows – a metaphor for emotions – as she lives with cancer. But she knows those are all creations of Thought. And that is how she has found freedom from her previous false god of cancer.

Who and what are your false gods? Who do you give power to?

It has been immensely helpful to know that it is the innocent creation of false gods that holds me back. And it is also so helpful – and hopeful – to know that every time I eliminate or wake up to a false god, I am reminded of the unified nature of my psychological experience. This unified place is where there is no splitting of Thought and feeling. Reawakened to the inside-out logic of how the mind works, I see that my feelings are residing in the home where they belong – in our spiritual home.

For me, this is not necessarily a religious place. It is a place of pure logic. Where potential arises. Where hope reigns supreme. Where resilience always exists. Where truth lives. And where one God resides.

BLOGSIGHT: *When we split Thought and feeling and believe that something or somebody else has power over our psychological or feeling state, it is as if we are handing over God's power to other multiple gods that do not actually exist. In so doing, we falsely assume our feelings to be coming from something other than Thought.*

Why Trying to Control
Thought Misses the Point

I was recently asked if we can manipulate Thought. I guess that's the game that modern psychology has been playing for quite some time now.

This question speaks to a deep-rooted misunderstanding that will one day shock the world to its very core as it becomes more and more obvious.

When we assume that the brain is the medium through which Thought runs, we begin to believe (quite reasonably, if this is our working hypothesis), that we can at least manipulate or control part of our emotional experience of life. Welcome to the world of affirmations, visualisation and positive thinking.

But a true understanding of the nature of Thought turns the entire discussion on its head. The biggest, most fundamental shift is to recognise that we are made of an essential nature or constant pre-existing intelligence called Mind. (You can come up with your own term to describe this "non-brain" force; specific words are not important here, though the principle we are speaking about absolutely is.) This Mind is the source of everything in the universe. And the brain is just one of its small operative parts.

As my close friend and mentor, Dicken Bettinger, writes in his book *Coming Home*:

> *"...What we are describing throughout this book is a new understanding of the source of experience. In this understanding, experience isn't created by your past, your personality, your biochemistry, your personality, other people, your circumstances, or even your thought content."*

At the beginning of the month, I had a pretty intense three weeks ahead of me: preparing the home and our family for the festival of Passover (ask any Jewish homemaker – very labour intensive!), make a brief transatlantic trip to South Africa to attend my nephew's Bar-Mitzvah celebrations, and single-handedly organise, just a few very short days later, my own son's Bar-Mitzvah featuring a sit-down dinner party for 130 people and a weekend of celebration and meals. To top it off, the day after the Bar-Mitzvah, we had our biggest work event of the year – the annual three-day Innate Health Conference!

Throughout this time, I felt mostly present, calm and available to do everything required for all these different events. I enjoyed each one immensely. This was not a feat of mine in any way. It was not about me or my capabilities. Really. It was just me being part of a profoundly predictable, reliable and generous setup that provides us with the resources to "do life". The Mind is not limited. It can cope with anything that shows up.

And then something unexpected occurred. Once these events were over, I faced an incident that may have been trivial for many others, but that I nonetheless struggled with. A messy mixture of hurt, disbelief and confusion, amongst other unwanted feelings, snuggled in and decided to stay for a while.

So I get to live with the whole gamut of experiences that my thinking creates: a real sense of presence and calm for a period, followed by a tsunami of uncomfortable feelings for another. But here's the point, the really essential, critical point:

All of it. Every bit of it. Last week, last year, this week, this year and ten years ahead will all be gifted to us from the same loving, reliable and giving source. It's a constant. No thought or idea we will ever think can be borne of a different origin. So we will be gifted an infinite amount of thoughts, ideas and, by extension, experiences as we go through our journey of life.

This understanding is truly precious. It lifts us out of analysing and keeping track of how we are doing, for we see that is simply unnecessary. Everything is working just as it needs to. There are no mistakes. No surprises. Just an inbuilt logic working one way, all of the time.

We are operating within a perfectly created paradigm. Our entire psychological, spiritual and emotional life is designed by a divine intelligence. And it is all-inclusive because you cannot create anything outside of this system. It's like a wave that thinks it is independent of the ocean. It may become bigger, crest and then fade, but whatever form it takes, it is always part of the infinite ocean and subject to its laws. Therefore, to even consider that "I will think positive" or "I will create good things with my mind" is using the power of Thought, which is a gift of Mind.

We can now become far more interested in the workings that I like to refer to as God-Mind – than in our own petty ego minds. And that is when life has the potential to make a lot more sense. When we can feel humble, safe and secure, even in the midst of our moment-to-moment struggles. When we can have complete faith in our innate health, our innate resilience, whatever we are feeling.

As we delve deeper into the perfection of the power of Thought, the idea of controlling it becomes illogical and foolhardy.

Manipulating Thought? It kind of misses the whole point.

BLOGSIGHT: *A true understanding of the nature of Thought informs us that we are operating within a pre-existing paradigm that cannot be controlled or changed. Our entire psychological, spiritual and emotional life derives from a single Intelligence that is all-inclusive.*

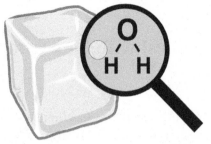

An ice cube   -   **Water**

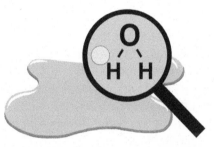

A puddle   -   **Water**

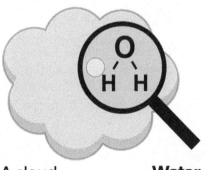

A cloud   -   **Water**

Being Honest with Our Emotions

If we could deeply appreciate the connection between Thought and feeling that alone would instantly change our experience of life. Nothing would ever be the same again.

I encourage people I care about (I usually begin with myself) to reflect on the truth of this fact again and again and again, on the one hundred percent truth of it. There is endless depth and understanding waiting to be found there.

I recently heard someone share the following: "Learning how my experience of reality is created from the inside-out has enabled me to become more honest with my emotions."

These words struck a chord with me. And they piqued my curiosity, as they remind me of the kind of conversation I have when people say to me, "I know that what I am going though and struggling with is essentially just Thought. But it doesn't help."

When we innocently fool ourselves, we get downhearted and assert that we know it's Thought but it's still not helping. But remember, it only works one way, one hundred percent of the time. It is just that we don't *really* believe it is Thought, which is *why* it is not helping. That's the good news.

One of the gifts of the inbuilt logic of learning about the single direction through which we experience and perceive life – from our minds, from the inside-out – is the knowledge that we can take complete accountability for our feelings. It's not rocket science. It's just common sense.

No one and nothing can make me feel anything. Ever. My emotions are always in sync with whatever I am thinking in the moment, whether I am aware of this or not. It's the way it works.

When I am in alignment with this truth, it frees me up to be honest with my feelings. I can own them as "my stuff". This in turn allows me to have those "hard conversations" I would otherwise avoid.

The old me – and the me that still sometimes forgets this truth – believed that frustration, irritation, insecurity and upset feelings were coming from others, or factors outside of me. Being so uncomfortable with my feelings explains why I was always reluctant to engage in dialogue when I was upset. But these days, as I have been fortunate to gain a small sense when I am "outside-in" (meaning, playing the blame game by attributing my feelings to something other than Thought), I more often, in the moment, feel a little "tap on the shoulder" when I am being tricked. Because if it is one hundred percent true that my feelings come and go within my own internal mental experience, then there cannot be any exceptions.

This line in the sand self-corrects us. It highlights the logic, differentiating between what *feels* to be true and what *is* actually true. There is no room for exceptions within a logical paradigm.

I sometimes hear people wishing that they never had *those* feelings anymore – the ones that don't feel good. But this is a misunderstanding of the nature of Thought and its connection to feeling.

We can be honest, confident and comfortable to feel *all* feelings when we are aligned with the logic of where they originate from. Everything is graciously welcomed in a mind that understands the way life is created. But very little can be tolerated in a mind that is built on misunderstanding.

So yes, I may be upset with you, but boy, is it helpful to know that I created that feeling from within me. This logic allows me to be above-board, honest and fair in my interactions.

And also very human.

> BLOGSIGHT: *Our emotions are always coming from our thinking in the moment, whether we are aware of this or not. This logic differentiates between what feels to be true and what is actually true. It is easy to have those hard but much-needed conversations and be honest with our feelings when we recognise where they originate from.*

All Thoughts Welcome – Come Inside

Chris Martin, lead singer of Coldplay, refers to Rumi's poem "The Guest House" as being the inspiration behind his new album, *A Head Full of Drums*, as well as a source of insight for navigating a challenging time in his life. This poignant poem tells a tale of the human condition.

This being human is a guest house.
Every morning a new arrival.

A joy, a depression, a meanness,
some momentary awareness comes
as an unexpected visitor.

Welcome and entertain them all!
Even if they're a crowd of sorrows,
who violently sweep your house
empty of its furniture,
still, treat each guest honourably.
He may be clearing you out
for some new delight.

The dark thought, the shame, the malice,
meet them at the door laughing,
and invite them in.

Be grateful for whoever comes,
because each has been sent
as a guide from beyond.

Last week, it felt as if a tidal wave of emotions was coursing through me, threatening to suck me under their gravitational pull. Certain events transpired – events which, if I had my choice, would not have occurred.

Before long, my ego mind was dancing, spinning and creating havoc in my sensory system. Feelings of hurt, anger and sadness nestled in my heart and mind. My unwanted feelings seemed to be birthed from these unwanted events. (Of course, the inside-out logic tells us this is not possible, but it sure *seemed* possible to me when I fell out of alignment with this understanding last week.)

I am often asked how a person should react when loved ones or friends seem to "hurt" them or "put them down". I do not believe there is a "should" answer to this question. But there is a fact that is always true whether we are awake to it or not.

No one can hurt us psychologically. No one can make us feel put down. It may look as if they can – but it is just not possible. Just like it's not possible for an elephant to fly, Dumbo aside. It goes against the grain of how things work. Here's the truth: hurt feelings come from hurt thinking. The feeling of being put down comes from "put down thinking".

Yes, someone can say hurtful things or derogatory things to you. But for you to experience the feeling of either of those, you need to have a thought. No feeling can exist outside of your capacity to think that feeling. Thought births it and Thought releases it. That is the only entry and exit point.

As Rumi's poem beautifully illustrates, we never know which "guests" will show up in the house of our minds. I sometimes like to deceive myself that I am "above" certain thoughts and feelings, impervious to feeling "affected" by someone else's behaviour. Or by life in general. But that is not the case. I, too, forget in the moment that no one and nothing has power over my heart and my mind. And so, without intending to, I fall head over heels. Not in love, but in hurt.

Each moment, when the true identity of these different guests – our feelings or emotions – is revealed, we can face the truth and invite all guests in with equal hospitality. There becomes no need to pull the blinds down on some guests while ushering others in with a smile. All guests can come and go in my house. They do anyhow. Whether I bury my head in the sand or not. It's just how the front entrance operates in my guest house. In all our guest houses.

So I sit patiently in my house and settle down on the slightly worn furniture. Slowly but surely, the raucous noise quiets down and the guests leave. They have spent almost a week here. Just as I realise they are spirit in disguise, they say goodbye and are gone.

Until the next time they come to visit…

BLOGSIGHT: *Thought gives birth to all feelings; it releases all feelings. As there is only one entry and exit point, no one can make us feel anything. It may look as if they can but it is just not possible. Hurt feelings come from hurt thinking.*

Our Innate Resilience – Look for What Is Already There

This past week, my four-year-old son Shaya really made me laugh. He wanted me to ask his fourteen-year-old brother to play with him. I knew it would probably be a futile endeavour anyhow. So my reply was straight out of the Bad Parenting Book 2.0:

"No."

He is a persistent young man however, so after unsuccessfully asking a few more times, he pulled me towards him and whispered in my ear, "Mommy, listen to the thoughts in your heart. They *want* to do this for me!"

He was right. They did. And I promptly set off to convince a highly ambivalent teenager to play with his four-year-old brother...

Yes, you could argue that little Shaya was pulling my strings, if that is even possible. (He is quite switched on!) But it was so fascinating to observe that though I have never directly spoken to him about the power of Thought, he is, by way of osmosis, picking up that our minds do change. We do not know what we will think. Right? In his world, that capacity lies in the heart.

What I love most about sharing the way the human experience works is that we are sharing what is already there. It is working independently of our awareness of it. We don't need to know about our built-in capacities in order to benefit from them. And once recognised, this knowledge feels so familiar, nothing more than common sense. It fits right, like a favourite pair of slippers.

When people come to learn at the Innate Health Centre for an individual or group session, they oftentimes can feel helpless, if not hopeless. A whole lot of confusion and misunderstandings may accompany them as they walk through the door. But when you look a little deeper, when you listen just beyond the panic, the hurt and the dissatisfaction, you slowly begin to see what is already there beneath the surface: a wonderful inbuilt resilience. It is always there.

Mind is an intelligence that gifts us the capacity to create experiences of our circumstances moment to moment via the power of Thought and Consciousness. This magical process is constantly and consistently regenerating and re-imagining life. It never runs out. It is solid and predictable. It is dependable and reliable. It is hard-wired into our psyche. And it is as part of us, as the roots are a part of a tree and the seasons are a part of nature's cycle.

For many years in my innocent and unintentional ignorance, I attributed these innate capacities to luck, chance, circumstance or any other haphazard reason that seemed feasible at the time. Thus, when I felt comfortable in my own skin (a rare occurrence in my teen years as I lived almost 24/7 in the feeling of constant self-conscious thinking), I automatically attributed it to something like losing weight or someone that "mattered" liking me, rather than an absence of self-conscious thinking.

I never recognised that I was having a deeper experience of being – of feeling my own innate resilience – and that's really all that accounted for the comfort factor. My moments of discomfort were nothing more than feeling the weather of my mind. But to me, it looked much more serious than that.

The first major "crisis" of my married life occurred when I miscarried during my first pregnancy. I was devastated, losing myself in a whirlpool of grief, despair and anger. I was convinced I would never get over this loss and never have children – a long-held fear of mine from my days of anorexia. Once again, I missed the always-available, inbuilt gift of the logic behind the working of the Mind.

And then, four weeks into my deep, post-miscarriage depression, a wise friend said something to me about God. I wasn't a big fan of God during this time, but that did not stop me from spontaneously having a profound, life-changing insight. A completely different understanding of the loss effortlessly emerged. Unsurprisingly, I suddenly felt emotionally and psychologically better.

But here's what you don't want to miss. For many years, I erroneously attributed this turnaround to the "wise person" who shared his thoughts with me, forgetting that he and others had said many wise, helpful things before, which had marginal, if any, impact on my life. At the time, I failed to recognise my own internal capacity to see something fresh in the moment from an organic place within me. If I had known its origin, it would have changed a lot for me. But I missed it and it took another ten years for me to realise its universal and constant nature.

Yes, our deeper, pristine essence might seem harder to notice than our perceived frailties. For these "frailties" are borne out of momentary manifestations of Thought and feeling, making them more likely to show up in our day-to-day experiences. They seem to jump out at us and cry for attention. Without much effort, these "imperfections" have a sneaky way of capturing our imagination.

No matter what we are going through, there is a deeper order that is working invisibly and seamlessly behind the scenes. Mind, Consciousness and Thought are always creating our psychological and spiritual experience. Each time we reawaken to their presence, we are reminded of a truth that is far greater than any personal truth we are able to conjure up ourselves.

I often have a moment, in the presence of my kids, husband, relatives, friends, colleagues, teachers, students and clients when I am touched and strengthened by their innate health. I recognise this not only when they are doing well, but also when they are struggling. This innate health is a constant, present in their pain as much as in their joy.

And I see it in myself as well, as I weather the storms of my mind or bathe in the gentleness and grace of life.

> BLOGSIGHT: *Mind gifts us the capacity to create experiences of our circumstances moment to moment via the power of Thought. This process is constant, working invisibly behind the scenes. Each time we reawaken to this fact, we are reminded of a truth that is far greater than any personal truth we are able to conjure up ourselves.*

Even in the Midst of an Earthquake, the Mind Is Simplicity

Mahima Shrestha is an inspirational woman and a good friend. At the time of the devastating Nepal earthquakes in April 2015, she was (and still is) a highly-regarded crisis management consultant to various large companies and organisations.

As the earthquake and its aftershocks suddenly ruptured her life and the lives of so many Nepalese citizens, Mahima had a moment of profound insight. At the actual moment of the earth literally splitting beneath her feet, Mahima's mind instantly filled with fear. But as her thoughts began to race about what to do, how to survive and how to help others, she had a life-changing realisation.

Mahima realised that everything she was feeling at that very moment was coming from Thought – *not* from what was happening outside of her. In other words, Mahima understood that the fear was completely separate to the circumstances, even the most extraordinary circumstances of multiple earthquakes striking her home and those she loved.

Now that's quite radical! Her life was in danger, that she won't dispute. Nonetheless, Mahima saw with stark clarity that *all* fear come from Thought. And when she saw this, her mind settled down, allowing her to feel peaceful, calm and fully present to help herself and others around her as best as she could.

Mahima conveys how this single but life-changing insight has had enormous ripple effects, impacting many areas of her life ever since. The story she shares is undoubtedly remarkable and inspiring. But even if you do not find yourself in the midst of an earthquake (I hope you don't!), there is so much to learn from what she realised in her moment of crisis.

Here is one key message to reflect on, as highlighted by Valda Monroe and Keith Blevens, who explain a crucial implication of learning about the inside-out logic of how the human experience works:

The future is an incomplete equation. As soon as we begin to imagine what will be or think into the future, however smart and prophetic we might believe ourselves to be, we will always be leaving out Thought in the moment. Because at that particular moment, when that particular situation actually arrives in our present lives, we will only be able to experience it through whatever thought comes to mind. We have no idea what that thought will be. So, by definition, the future becomes an incomplete equation. And imagining it is pretty much a waste of our emotional and psychological energy.

When we see this logic for what it is, it takes a lot off our minds. It settles us down into enjoying and navigating our present-day lives with its entire vicissitudes; all its ups and downs – the unexpected and the expected.

"The Mind is simplicity" Sydney Banks stated in his inimitable way. He saw life from where it begins. From its basic elements. From its source.

This Mind is pure, pre-existing intelligence. The power of Thought is the vehicle connecting us to this deeper world of wisdom, love, compassion, respect, humility, gratitude, harmony, perspective and quiet. All knowledge resides here. This is what Mahima uncovered in such extraordinary circumstances.

BLOGSIGHT: *The future is an incomplete equation because as soon as we begin to imagine what will be or think into the future, we will always be leaving out Thought in the moment. When a particular situation actually arises, we will only be able to experience it through whatever thought comes to mind at that moment. We have no idea what that thought will be until we have it.*

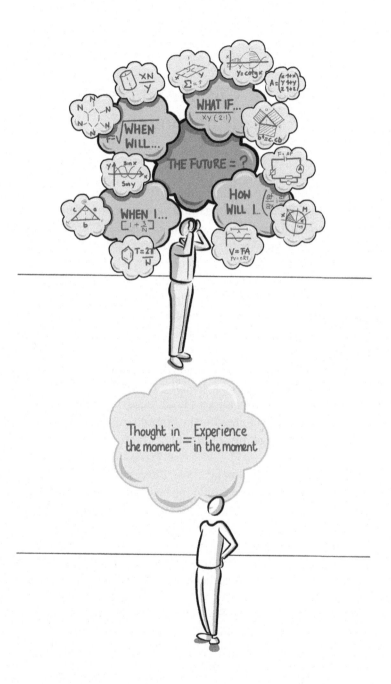

Are Our Circumstances Also Made of Thought?

All our thinking moments are notes that play together as a universal song. And if we listen beneath the empty, tinny, superficial noise of our mental chatter, we can sometimes hear and understand a far deeper message of knowledge and truth. This is the depth, purity and source of all Thought and all experience.

Is it possible that the same hidden depth lies beneath our circumstances? If there is an intelligence powering every organism in the universe, is it not worth considering that this same intelligence is powering *all* circumstances – even the seemingly mundane, insignificant ones?

Three years ago, when I was very ill for a period of time, I came to realise that my body had been speaking to me. What began as a soft, intelligent whisper, morphed into a bold request and finally, a piercing scream. And yet, I had steadfastly ignored my body's increasingly desperate attempts to get my attention.

Why?

Because at the time, I was far more interested in the thoughts that seemed to speak to me from inside my head, via words, constructs and language. It is embarrassing to admit, but I honestly did not realise the significance of the relationship between mind and body. Somehow, I had missed recognising that the body also speaks.

This was a poignant and profound learning message for me. It woke me up to the inescapable and crucial mind-body connection, an insight which moved me very deeply at the time. I sobbed when it hit me how I had disrespected my body's voice for so long, and how I had disregarded its urgent warnings. But I was deeply grateful that it had spoken so loudly, such that I could not ignore it any longer. To this day, appreciating and recognising the relationship between my mind and body remains an ongoing learning experience for me.

One of the ideas that the Three Principles brings to life is that there is a deeper utterance behind every movement in the universe. Every action has the power of Thought behind it. Every tear spilt is brought to life via Consciousness. Every sentiment is crafted from the intelligence of Mind.

So this begs a critical question: what about our day-to-day circumstances? Is there also meaning in the apparently trivial ones, like getting a parking ticket or winning praise from our boss? And what about the deeply challenging ones such as relationship troubles, bereavement, illness and the many other "big" issues that we inevitably come face to face with in our lives?

Well, here's the way I relate to this question: the circumstances of our lives are borne of the power of Thought also.

These circumstances (just another term for describing everything that is happening to and around us all of the time) are made up of the divine fabric that creates Thought. And they are intelligently brought to life via universal Consciousness.

We have somehow fallen into the error of perceiving circumstances as separate, as forces independent of us. Even those of us who see Mind, Thought and Consciousness as the elements creating our psychological experience of life, struggle to avoid falling into this very subtle, well-laid "trap". So it seems as if there is the inside world from which we create our experience. And then there is the outside world with the stuff that happens to us.

We therefore assume that our circumstances are random events with little meaning. We trust that we can relate to them via the power of Thought and find meaning that way. And yes, it is undeniable that the capacity to find intrinsic meaning is empowering. It is truth. But I don't think it is the whole truth. There is more to this story.

Our circumstances speak to us just as our minds and bodies speak to us. We can hear their sounds via the power of Thought. They are borne of the same underlying messages and are part of the universal song being played. Their notes may sound discordant, even catastrophic at times. But nonetheless, we cannot escape the fact that they are part of the vocal chords of the universe.

The universe sings one song. Its voice is heard through nature, through people and through events and circumstances. Sometimes though, the volume may be turned down in our minds. We do not hear it because we forget to listen carefully, as I did when my body desperately tried to engage me in conversation. Or we interpret the events through our own bias and judgment, inevitably missing the deeper utterances. We hear the words but we don't hear the message.

It is so reassuring to know that there is intrinsic meaning to every dimension of life, whether that meaning is concealed or revealed. It is always there, ever-present, woven perfectly into the fabric of the universe, though often it remains hidden in its garments.

Sydney Banks profoundly expressed that "nothing on the outside can hurt you, nothing on the outside can help you, because there is no outside".

Nothing can exist without Thought. I do not believe this excludes circumstances.

> BLOGSIGHT: *We have fallen into the error of perceiving circumstances as separate, independent forces. It seems as if there is an inside world from which we create our experience and an outside world with the stuff that happens to us. But as nothing can exist without Thought, it must be that the circumstances of our lives are also borne of Thought.*

Learning from the Next Generation

A charming fictional dragonfly named Curious is the animated inspiration of John Scott (our very own illustrator of this book!) and Stephanie Fox. As a winged insect trying to make his way in the big, wide world, Curious has moments when he gets scared, anxious and insecure. Doing his best to push these emotions away, Curious looks to find "better" feelings outside of himself by engaging in activities that in the past seemed to engender the kind of experience he craves. But it doesn't work. As hard as he tries, Curious just cannot seem to find the feelings he so desires.

This is because Curious does not yet know that as he thinks, his reality is constructed. He has not yet understood that his feelings are a reflection of his own consciousness, coming to life through his moment-to-moment thinking, which has nothing to do with the outside world.

Last week, the Innate Health Centre's "Mental Health Resilience and Recovery" seminar featured a panel of young people far wiser than Curious, even wiser than the majority of grown-ups who, much like Curious, often fail to see the universal, invisible, creative power behind their perception and feeling of the world. Allow me to introduce a few of these panellists:

Naimh is eight years old. She already understands how we feel and see our world through Thought. It has helped her deal with so-called-bullying behaviour with a grace and maturity far beyond her years. Naimh's appreciation for the nature of Thought has also been crucial in enabling her to move beyond her own terror when tackling her first Alton Towers rollercoaster ride. This amazing young lady's self-developed insight is that "Mind is the power source behind the brain". She is quite something!

Alysia, age eleven, bravely overcame her phobia of throwing up. As she came to recognise the inside-out logic that explained her irrational fear, she saw how it was the "thought" (her word) of being sick that was causing her to be fearful. This insight helped Alysia to get over a very difficult time in her life and was the crucial element in her healing.

Fourteen-year-old Akiva delivered his public-speaking presentation at school on the Three Principles of Innate Health. Armed with what he now knows about how human beings operate, Akiva feels equipped to face an unexpected recent challenge: his parents and the rest of his family choosing to live abroad while he finishes school in London. "My stress around this issue comes from my thinking", says Akiva. "Because I know that, I can handle this."

Liora is twenty-one and, in her own words, a "recovering perfectionist". She has begun to see through the labels she and others created for herself, realising that these were created from Thought. The lid is off her "box", which she now sees is nothing more than a creation of the mind. And so, her mind is free to insightfully give her out-the-box thinking that didn't seem to previously exist. Liora is now far less interested in analysing her thinking (that comes pretty easily to a final-year mathematics student) and is allowing herself to experience, feel and get over things with a freedom that she has not known in a long while.

I am sure none of these young people would profess to be the perfect psychological package. In fact, they don't seem to care about that at all (even Liora, the recovering perfectionist!); it is just not on their radar. These remarkable and yet very ordinary young women and men are simply inspired and delighted to know that there is a constant and predictable logic explaining all of their experience.

So Naimh, Alysia, Akiva, Liora and so many other young people rest secure in knowing they have the keys to the castle, guaranteed entry by the natural process of ongoing psychological learning.

They are free to struggle and triumph, knowing that both options are equally accounted for by the Mind. Neither lies outside the remit of the divine.

The 'how you're doing' board

They grab onto the wonder and awe that a power exists to create all of their experience. And they are under no illusions that there will be times when they will forget about this power. Because when it does happen, they tend to find it curious (hence the name of the animated star of this blog) and a little scary sometimes. Not dangerous or indicative of failure. These young people are therefore free to stumble over their misunderstandings and learn from them. According to our feedback forms, they, more than any of the other adult speakers and panellists, inspired and enthused our mental health professionals last week.

My heart lies with educating the younger generation. Most of them have not yet bought in to the unhelpful preoccupation with "how we are doing". They don't care to judge their moods and score points when they are "doing well". And they do not need to deduct points when they are not doing well. (Not "scoring" ourselves? Now there's something for those of us who are a bit older to learn!)

Young people have a natural tendency to look outwards to learn from the world, rather than inwards at themselves. This is what being curious truly means. With this new map of understanding that explains how we create our reality close at hand, so many of the young people that I have met now feel more confident than ever to go out into the world and be themselves.

It is delightful and inspiring – and should fill us all with immense hope.

BLOGSIGHT: *As we think, we feel. Our feelings are therefore a reflection of our moment-to-moment thinking. This has nothing to do with the outside world, freeing us up to experience all kinds of feelings, knowing that all options are equally accounted for by the Mind.*

Free to Be Me – The Story of an Eleven-Year-Old Girl

Hannah is painfully shy. Although we have known each other for a long time – since she was a newborn baby in fact – Hannah has rarely uttered more than a few sentences to me. Hannah not only struggles to express herself, but tends to withdraw into her own world, which most likely seems safer and more understanding than the world we clumsy adults are capable of offering her.

So it took me by surprise when this little angel of a girl unexpectedly asked to speak with me recently. Hannah arrived looking absolutely terrified, as if, on second thoughts, this was a really bad idea. When I asked what she wanted to talk about, she panicked momentarily and ran out to call her mother who subsequently sat with us while we spoke.

After a few minutes, Hannah settled down and a slow but steady stream of thoughts began to flow. She described the special needs school she attends and her conviction that the teacher "doesn't like me." This teacher, in her mind, seemed to think she was antagonistic (my word), ungrateful (her word) and uncooperative (my word).

This was surprising to hear as I had long known Hannah to be introverted, wary and careful not to make too much of a fuss lest she gets unduly noticed. Hannah further expressed how she finds it difficult to make eye contact and how angry her teacher seems to become when this occurs. Hannah also related her resistance to her teacher's demand that she join up with the younger class for a term. When the teacher told Hannah she was being difficult, Hannah countered that she considered it "babyish to be with the babies." (Not exactly a ridiculous observation, is it?)

What was most surprising to me was that this quiet and apparently unconfident little girl was digging her heels in and standing her ground.

Hannah was, in her words, "fighting with my teacher". I was so proud of Hannah, deeply touched by her self-belief that she could and should have a say.

When it was my turn to speak, I shared with Hannah my belief that she has a secret but powerful gift given to her by God. (Hannah comes from a religious family so this kind of reference was appropriate for her.) All human beings have this gift, but sometimes we don't know we have it. "It is planted deep within our souls," I told Hannah. I could tell this meant something to her.

I explained to Hannah that she had the power to find a place in her mind, heart and soul where despite her teacher getting crazy with her, she can be OK. I asked Hannah if it would be helpful to discover this secret place inside herself.

"Do you mean I can be me?" she asked.

I wanted to cry. Instead, I told her that was exactly what I meant. "Yes, you can be you, even while your teacher gets angry."

Hannah relaxed instantly as she considered how this would feel. A profound conversation ensued during which we discussed having experiences that do not always go as we would like and meeting people who don't "get us". And the very reasonable expectation that it is OK to be ourselves even so.

I sensed how something that until then had looked impossible began dissolving in Hannah's mind. In its place, hope arose. A trail of thought disappeared as a new trail began to emerge.

I now have a confession to make. Earlier in the week, I had become aware that someone I admired had taken issue with me. All week this had been playing on my mind. I felt betrayed (who says I still don't venture into drama?) and pained (see what I mean?) that someone who "matters" to me could utter such "mean" and "untrue" sentiments.

Nonetheless, I did my best to keep myself above the turbulent thoughts swimming inside my head. I recognised where my feelings were coming from, and for the most part, let my ego mind ramble on without paying too much attention to it. But I was still struggling. Cue an eleven-year-old, painfully shy young girl and an unexpected conversation.

People often ask me who the best teachers of this understanding are. (As if it is some kind of competition in which contestants get ranked and rated.) Well, if you are open to learning, you will find teachers everywhere. Only they show up in all different guises.

Hannah's endearing bravery, openness and steadfast commitment to follow her own path conveyed a profound and important message to me. Here I am – a so-called grown-up – fully able to defend myself and hold my own. Hannah, on the other hand, is still a child, limited in the ability to express herself, very tentative in the world of social interactions and seemingly lacking in confidence. Yet she was willing to look at this inner gift to be herself and let others be themselves. Guided by Hannah's courage, I once again was reawakened to this gift for myself.

In a relatively short conversation, an extraordinary young girl created a little bit of heaven for herself in the midst of what seemed like a raging battlefield. And I too woke up, once again, to that place of heaven inside of me.

> BLOGSIGHT: *The purity of Mind allows Thought, the creative agent that guides us through life, to do just that. It allows us to create anything and everything; to be ourselves and let others be themselves.*

Resilience Revisited

Not long ago, I began working with a lovely young teenager named Diana who was going through a very difficult time. In vividly describing how she was very needy of attention, Diana, in her own words, told me that she was "low on love".

Diana expressed how she had felt let down by a lot of people in her life. She shared how all her current dysfunctional behaviours stemmed (at least, in her mind) from this gaping vacuum inside her, always "too deep and too wide too fill." It saddened me to hear how alone Diana felt, how she was attempting to fill her loneliness in ways that seemed to create more of the very feeling she wanted to get rid of. But at the same time, I felt reassured at how misleading this was.

It struck me when listening to Diana that "low on love" was a thought she had carried around for a long time. It emerged from an innocent misunderstanding at a moment in her life when it looked to be true. This thought had been innocently nurtured into a belief that had given birth to many more thoughts that reinforced its heavy and loaded message. These supporting thoughts were all the evidence Diana needed. They bore witness to this "truth" of hers and rejected anything that seemed unaligned with that truth.

Diana's story was a heavy weight for her to bear. I could immediately envisage some of the feelings that would invariably flow from the weight of this story:

Resentment and hurt: "They don't care about me."

Disappointment: "They let me down again."

Loneliness: "There is no one who understands me or whom I trust to love me like I need to be loved."

I shared with Diana how each time these thoughts came to mind for her, Consciousness would bring it to life as a feeling. Because Diana thought it, she had to feel it.

Diana had never entertained that "low on love" had been borne of mere energy, and had thus crept into her mind and heart out of a simple misunderstanding. We discussed the origins of "low on love." How it sneaked in when Diana felt "let down" by her distracted parents (her words) for the first time. She assumed that they were responsible for the empty feeling inside, not realising that it was actually the quiet voice of Thought whispering to her and creating a reaction of feelings in her sensory system. Each time her trust was broken by a friend or a loved one, Diana mistakenly assumed that the rejection and emptiness came from them. Each time, a notch was added on the belt of "low on love" until it threatened to strangle her if she didn't do something.

Diana did not realise that the feelings were coming from Thought and not from other people. If she had realised this, the taut belt would have immediately slackened, allowing her to breathe in her own pure oxygen. She would have experienced resilience in place of loneliness.

Resilience is revealed when misunderstanding falls away. It gifts us the strength and insight to respond to life when our expectations are not met. When people seem cruel. When we feel betrayed. When we feel ignored. Unheard. Misunderstood.

Resilience always hears us. It is our inner fortress. Resilience lies at the heart of all Thought and feeling. While it cannot always be felt, it is always there. It is a most faithful servant.

As we spoke, I shared with Diana how I sometimes behave in similar ways to her parents when interacting with my children. I don't listen. I don't attend to them when they need me to. I don't fully understand them. I judge them. Yet it has so far never occurred to my kids that they are "low on love". Rather, they move towards assuming that "mom is busy", or "mom just doesn't get it", or some other explanation that their resilience offers them at that particular moment.

I also conveyed how it seems to be part of life's design that human beings are fallible and living in their own reality. They therefore do not necessarily align with our wants, needs and expectations, however reasonable these expectations may seem to us. Our needs, and others' reactions to our needs, can be way out of sync. Both are borne out of Thought in the moment. And both occur in different people's minds in different ways. To rely on other people's behaviour is like stepping onto the water and expecting to walk across it – not possible even if you are a world-class magician like David Blaine!

Now here's the good news: but for the thought "low on love", Diana can absolutely be filled with a river of love. This is an implication of being in harmony with the truth of where love, trust and other deeper feelings lie as a constant. They are not contingent on the outside world. No one can give them to us or take them away from us. It doesn't work that way.

Indeed, as our conversations unfolded, it was a privilege to watch this wonderful young woman's mind begin to expand, when she realised that feeling low on love was no longer the absolute truth she has believed it to be for so long.

BLOGSIGHT: *Resilience is revealed as misunderstanding falls away. Nothing needs to be done to access our innate resilience – it is always there. This provides us with the confidence, trust and insight to respond to the outside world.*

Who Poisoned My Mind?

Here is what I love about the Principles of the Mind: it is a learning that is foundational – not personal. These Principles are therefore evident in all of life, not only in my life. What I mean is that the same Intelligence that powers my ability to think, powers the world of nature and of all human psychology and physiology.

A friend and colleague recently referred to insights he gleaned from *The Secret of the Trees*, a book that documents how trees communicate with each other. Intrigued, I looked into this fascinating topic myself. Here is what I discovered:

Acacia trees, upon sensing giraffes or other animals browsing from their leaves, begin producing leaf tannin in quantities lethal to the browsers. This so-called poison changes the taste of the leaves, making it bitter and unpalatable to the browsers. Remarkably, the tree then sends an "alarm signal" to all other trees within a fifty-metre radius, warning them of impending danger. These other trees respond by producing their own leaf tannin within five to ten minutes.

Now, if this is not incredible in its own right, it is even more extraordinary to discover that giraffes quickly catch on to what is happening. The giraffes begin to avoid the trees in the immediate area and also alert other members of the herd as to which trees are safe to eat from.

A researcher stumbled onto this discovery when he was investigating the sudden death of some 3,000 antelope, called kudu, on game ranches in the eastern part of South Africa. He noticed that giraffe, roaming freely, browse only on one acacia tree in ten, avoiding those trees that are downwind. Kudu however, which are fenced in on the game ranches, have little to eat other than acacia leaves during the winter months. So these antelope continue to browse until the tannin from the leaves sets off a lethal metabolic chain reaction in their bodies. The kudu, so it seems, have little options due to being fenced in. The only alternative is to starve.

So many times in life we erroneously feel that we have no options. Outside factors limit us, forcing us to react to them within the confines of set parameters. We feel poisoned not by acacia trees but by people behaving badly, by unfair criticism and judgement, overwhelming work and family demands, deadlines, expectations of ourselves and others, day to day "pressures of life", and many other external factors. And yes, all of these factors do indeed exist. After all, we live in a world of people (all of whom are annoyingly fallible), work and family issues, deadlines, illness – overall, a very dynamic, "lots-of-stuff-happening" life.

However, when we realise that the "poison" in our minds is not injected into us by these outside factors or circumstances, but is instead connected to our thinking in the moment, it frees our minds to listen to the Intelligence that informs and takes care of us. It takes care of everything, the giraffes *and* the trees. No one is left out of its infinite embrace. This Intelligence holds all things, at all times.

For the trees, this shows up as emitting poison to protect themselves. They are so responsive to this Intelligence that they even have the awareness to alert their fellow trees about the issue at hand. For the giraffes, it means that they recognise it is not safe to eat the bitter leaves. So they make a plan. (I can't imagine that they moan about how unfair it all is, but who knows, maybe this is a new idea for a Gary Larson *Far Side* comic strip?) Unfortunately for the hemmed-in kudu, they can't save themselves, as humans have intruded and interfered with their natural habitat.

Make no mistake, God's system is watertight. The deeper workings of the mind are perfectly responsive to life. They are designed for life. It is human misunderstanding that creates errors.

When we think that it is the external factors in life that makes us feel a certain way, we function in a misunderstanding that, though innocent, is not logical, true, or accurately reflective of how things actually work. And by the way, blaming ourselves is no different to blaming outside factors. We are *also* an outside factor!

This misunderstanding has practical implications. For the trees there is the threat of their impending demise if they cannot come up with a "solution" to being ravaged by these giant creatures. For the giraffes, they may continue to eat the bitter leaves, "hoping" it gets better as they constantly digest more toxins. But fortunately for both, they intrinsically grasp how life is informed. They listen differently. They listen within – to Thought in the moment, to the inner voice of Consciousness.

So it seems that we humans have a lot to learn from the giraffes and the acacia trees. In fact, much of the time, I find (somewhat disconcertedly) that I am far more in line with the kudu. But I am not fenced in literally. I am fenced in by my own misunderstandings about where my experience is coming from.

Knowing we are only ever a thought away from insight helps to take away the anxiety that anything from the outside can harm us psychologically. It removes the false assumption that there are no options other than a poisoned mind.

The answers lie in the same place – always.

BLOGSIGHT: *The Mind – like nature – works in a logical, predictable and reliable way. It is human misunderstanding that creates errors. When we think that it is the external factors in life that makes us feel a certain way, we function in a misunderstanding that is not logical or reflective of how things actually work.*

Is Your Life Based on a True Story?

I recently picked up the latest book by the well-known illusionist, Derren Brown, *Happy – why more or less everything is absolutely fine*. While I don't agree with everything the author writes, I appreciate that he takes a reflective and philosophical look at the deeper workings of the mind and reality. At the beginning of the book, Derren draws an astute comparison between the perspective we hold when we watch a movie that is based on a true story and the lack of perspective we often have when living the biopic of our own lives. Even while watching a movie based on facts, we realise that there is artistic licence helping to shape the story. We take into account that it's not about the specific details (not *all* of it will be true) but more about the bigger picture. However, when trapped inside our own heads, we often take what we see and experience as the absolute truth of how things actually are.

Derren insightfully quotes Arthur Schopenhauer: "Every man takes the limits of his own field of vision for the limits of the world."

We don't realise how we constantly edit, erase and join the dots to create our own vision or version of life. This is hugely significant, because if we understand how life works from the inside-out, we will view it very differently to when we fall into misunderstanding about the same situation. In other words, the way we understand life in each moment influences us to join the dots in different ways.

Illusionists like Derren Brown skillfully take advantage of our naivety or lack of knowledge of how we think reality is being created. When we are outside-in, we will assume the illusionist has a lot of power that he doesn't actually have! But when we are inside-out, we are secure and realise that Derren is not actually creating an illusion. This allows us to be curious.

Understanding how our perceptions are created at their roots creates the potential for us to become humble. And in that newfound humility, we can discover that we are actually seeing the world through our own thinking minds; that there is infinite knowledge in every moment that lies outside of what we currently think, see and know. For example, how many times do we later realise that what we thought about a certain event was only part of the story? We were missing bits; we may have misunderstood or even unintentionally edited and erased bits.

It is extremely freeing to know that while our current thoughts about our pasts tell a story that we have lived, they also create and construct their own narrative. This narrative is our version of the story. The way we have joined up the dots. Dot to dot. Thought by thought. Once again this will always depend on where we sit in the logic of how life works.

This is why our pasts sometimes seem to change, and that leads to the crucial question: if our past has happened already, why is it not set in stone? While the events of our past may be fixed, how is it that our experience of them can shift and change, sometimes almost effortlessly?

The answer is simple. When the dots join up differently (another way of saying we have a fresh look or an insight into the past), it can and will change our pasts from our present. This resolution is not the end of the story. But it does mean that the past no longer has the power to dictate how we feel in the present moment. This is incredible!

I know from over four decades of living that there are many hidden threads of Thought that I hold about myself. These have woven ingrained stories to which I am often completely oblivious. I am sure they play out, day in and day out. But does it really matter? Not to me. Because the only means through which we get to create our stories is through Thought, I have learned that I can only do the best I can with what occurs to me in any given moment. But crucially, it isn't the whole story.

It always fascinates me when I see how I create judgement or forgiveness about the same person, based purely on how I join the dots at a specific moment. Both have radically different outcomes – not necessarily for the other person, but definitely for me. Judgement feels awful. Forgiveness feels wonderful. Yet judgement always seems to justify itself. The dots of my thinking join up like those dot-to-dot books I loved as a kid and make it feel like that's what's really there.

But what would happen if we knew Thought is the way we create reality, rather than reality itself? If we knew that Thought is our feeling about reality rather than an inherent quality in reality itself?

In the moments when we are aware that we are seeing life as it appears to us, through our own joining of the dots, we will be less dogmatic and more humbled. We will also be able to listen with more respect to others, knowing that they too are seeing us, themselves and life through their own joined-up dots. Knowing that there is always a wider lens of perception provides more freedom. When our narrative stops being the only true story in our minds and instead becomes "the way we see it right now", we are more likely to feel a lightness and openness. We have less on our minds.

For me, it is the difference between how I feel when I see a film that is based on truth (it weighs on me as I think about how people actually went through that in real life) and one that is fiction (I forget about it quicker; it's more along the lines of, *Wow, what an amazing and creative mind behind that story!*) Both are entertaining. But the former feels entrenched, limited and heavy, while the latter is freeing, creative and limitless.

So the point is not to question whether what we are thinking is true or not true. Rather, it is to know that we have been given the extraordinary gift to join the dots of our lives into a story. And to understand the truth of how reality works and how it does not. Who wouldn't want to know that?

And finally, we can begin to see the cosmic humour in how we all seem to think we are pretty darn good at them – these dot-to-dot pictures. It's nice to know we are all still playing in the kindergarten classroom.

BLOGSIGHT: *Our story about ourselves can never be the full story. When we are living with awareness that we are only ever seeing life as it appears to us in each moment, we realise that our minds can instantly change. We also begin to listen with more respect to others, knowing that they too are seeing life through their own experience of Thought in the moment.*

Why the Habitual, Addictive Cycle *Can* Be Broken

The Little Book of Big Change – the no-willpower approach to breaking any habit challenges the assumption that we need willpower to break our ingrained habits and addictions. (This applies whether we label them "behavioural" or "thought habits".) Because so many of us have not yet found a solution to breaking or dissolving our habits, it feels like they are here forever. But based on her understanding of the logic of the Three Principles, author Amy Johnson gives hope to those who assume that these habits are now entrenched and immutable facets of their personalities and lives.

I can definitely relate to this assumption.

I used to suffer from extreme food bingeing, feeling helpless in the face of my compulsion to eat anything and everything I could get my hands on. There is nothing pretty or graceful about a binge, whether its food, alcohol, drugs or any other form of sedative. They are all "designed" to take away an incredibly compelling urge that feels extremely frightening and uncomfortable. Based on her own research as an MD, Amy explains the biological and neurological pathways created by the misunderstanding at the root of where the habit begins. She also explains how these pathways are instantly uprooted and rewired when the misunderstanding that is keeping the habit in place falls away and insight emerges.

If you are unaware of this, it often seems as if you have no control or ability to resist the urges of your habitual or addictive behaviour. You assume you will be stuck with them forever. At best, you resign yourself to endless, interminable battles that – if you were a betting person – you wouldn't back yourself to win most times.

I remember explaining to many therapists how impotent I felt once an urge seemed to overtake me. It was as if I was possessed by a power greater than me. I seemed to lose myself – and then find myself again hours later, ashamed and so very disappointed by my "abject failure". To compound matters, the huge misunderstanding that I was at the mercy of some seemingly unstoppable addictive force was not challenged by the people I looked to for help. They also misunderstood the nature of the cycles I was trapped in and encouraged me to use willpower and manipulation of my mind to fight these demons, which simply amplified the problem.

Amy explains how willpower can never ultimately win these battles. Even at my lowest points – when I was so confused and desperate – I knew this was true. Because the one thing you would not have called me was lazy. I was up for a fight. A good one. Yet I always seemed to lose, each and every time.

How did these addictive habits first appear on our psychological radar? At a certain point in our past, we attempted to get rid of an uncomfortable feeling or find a nicer feeling. In our delusion and innocence, a "new" habit seemed the quickest way to give us relief. Which it usually did, at least for a short while. But we quickly got hooked. We temporarily felt safe as we found a way to sedate the pain and deal with unwanted feelings.

Obsessive thinking and addictive behaviours can momentarily and superficially distract us. But they will never be genuinely satisfying. And they will not give us the solution we are looking for. Actually, they simply become a vicious cycle.

It will never be satisfying, because the feeling – whether painful or beautiful – is not coming from the outside. And so, it cannot be dealt with from the outside. All feeling, whether positive or negative, derives and comes alive through the power of Thought.

It is incredibly helpful to know that our habits are not rooted in our personalities, our DNA, or our pasts. We have a capacity to live in and sit with uncomfortable feelings when we remember that they too are created from the power of Thought; the power that creates all of our experience. Every time we see the Thought-feeling connection – which tells us that all our feelings and impulses are created from the power of Thought – it becomes more and more obvious that food, alcohol, getting "likes" on Facebook, and so many other emotional and psychological needs we wish to have met, cannot put a feeling in us. This is the beginning of finding freedom from addictive behaviours and thought patterns.

The Mind is a deep spiritual and psychological resource. There is nothing outside of its remit. It is replete with infinite knowledge and wisdom. And we are a part of this knowledge and wisdom. Each time we realise and remember the truth of how our habits and feelings are created or are not created, false barriers to this wisdom fall away and deeper feelings of wholeness are revealed.

So no, I don't binge like I used to in the past – it's been over twenty-five years since. But yes, I still forget where my feelings are coming from on a daily basis. And when I forget, I still look to food and other distractions to help me out. But the power they once held over me is no longer. Because every time, in that moment when I once again wake up to the origin of where real power lies, of where feelings come from, there is a resetting of sorts.

We now know the singular source of misunderstanding that has created, does create and will create all addictions and habits. Armed with this knowledge, we are light years ahead of the rest of the field. We can break the cycles that we assumed could never be broken – no matter how hard we tried.

BLOGSIGHT: *Habits and addictions are our best attempt to deal with uncomfortable feelings. But feelings are a creation of Thought in the moment. Overcoming them is therefore not a battle of willpower, but an awakening to the power of Thought and its relationship to the feelings that led to these addictive behaviours in the first place.*

Fatigue Killer – Too Tired to Think

For almost as long as I can remember, fatigue and I have had a fascinating relationship. In my teenage years we were lovers, in my twenties we were enemies, in my thirties a truce was signed, and now, in my early forties, we have reconnected as good friends.

There was a time, back when I was a young mother of a (very) fast-growing family, when tiredness and suffering seemed completely intertwined. If I was tired, I was going to suffer... and so my story went. The impact of fatigue on my level of well-being felt real and inescapable. I assumed that being exhausted meant that I was under-resourced, which fully "justified" my feelings of irritability, stress and overwhelm. I eventually became so frightened of tiredness that I fell headfirst into a decade-long battle with sleep, or lack of it. Before long, I found myself caught in the interminable cycle of insomnia and sleeping pills. Fatigue became my enemy.

One day in my late twenties, I found myself complaining to a new acquaintance how I had not slept for more than a three hour stretch in three years due to severely colicky babies and toddlers who couldn't yet read a clock. (I wasn't exaggerating – five little people under the age of seven lived in my house at the time!)

My friend acknowledged that she too hadn't slept in a long time and was also exhausted. However, when she spoke about her fatigue, it did not sound like such a big deal to her. This shocked me! As I got to know her better (in the hope of stealing her kryptonite!), I saw how my friend did indeed look very tired – like me – but was not irritable and down about it – unlike me. Fatigue was not strangling her as it was strangling me. I wondered why it was kinder to her.

It was then that my mind (that brilliant genius of a companion I live with) gifted me a memory of ten years previously, a flashback to the days when I was an adventurous and slightly rebellious teenager. I had stayed up many a night – sometimes all night – to party, have deep heart-to-heart conversations with friends, or study for exams. Going on adrenaline, I had a blast, even when faced with a full and busy day ahead of me. I seemed able to dive into life – fatigue and all!

This memory caused me to pause and reflect. I realised the difference was not that I was now a decade older, but that back then I did not have the belief that tiredness could limit me. So it didn't. It occurred to me that somewhere along the way, I had assumed that fatigue held an inexorable, manifest power over me. So it did. If you think it's true it *is* true for you.

Seeing my innocent mistake led to a self-correction.

The discriminator is always this: *where do I think my feelings of psychological exhaustion and deflation are coming from?*

When I mistakenly assume it comes from fatigue, I seem to grab it with both hands. But when I insightfully realise that this is not true – as the inside-out logic of the mind does not work this way – my spirits and presence of mind have the potential to soar. It is then that I can find myself extremely tired physically, yet often very alert, highly creative and exceptionally energised. This does not mean that I do not still get tired. (Did I mention that I am exhausted as I write this blog, after getting just three hours sleep last night?) But as I delve deeper into the power of the Mind and recognise that it functions independently of outside variables, my entire relationship to fatigue is subject to change – even when I am very tired.

Now, don't get me wrong. The body and mind are connected; we are physical beings, so we need to sleep and take care of ourselves. Thank goodness that our minds provide us, via the power of Thought, with both the common sense and insight needed to look after our physical well-being. (Whether we listen to it or not is another thing – I can be really stubborn sometimes!)

But what surprised me back then is that when I insightfully realised that fatigue was *not* the enemy surrounding and holding my spirits to ransom, I began to experience more freedom in the face of it. And so my resilience, in the face of being extremely tired, spontaneously surfaced.

When we think fatigue is holding us back
(outside-in).

Realising our experience of fatigue is created through Thought
(inside-out).

To wit: previously, I would have arrived at the Innate Health Centre to teach an evening class after a long day of work broken up only by a two hour check-in with the kids, thinking "there is no way I can be of help to anyone here who is past their first birthday". Now, while I still find myself coming up against the exact same practical scenario, these thoughts feature far less. Consequently, as I begin teaching, my fatigued self all but disappears from my mind. Before I know it, I am engaged, energised, present and clear-headed.

Nonetheless, I have a confession to make. I sometimes still moan about being tired just as I moan about the weather. (Moaning seems to be what we do as responsible adults!) But I can no longer take my experience of fatigue as seriously as I once did. It has changed. Radically. So now, despite my moaning, I really do *not* mind when my fatigue joins me at my four-year-old's bed time, for a full day and evening of teaching and work, or even for a bout of exercise at the gym. It's welcome.

I used to think I would look forward to the day when fatigue took leave of me. (I was told that does eventually happen when all the kids finally leave home.) But now I am not so sure. We have become friends. Solid friends.

BLOGSIGHT: *The discriminator is always where we think our feelings are coming from. As the power of the Mind functions from the inside-out, independently of outside variables, it is a mistake to assume our feelings come from fatigue or any other factor.*

Judge, Jury and Executioner – Giving Judgement the Lethal Injection

Judgement eats away at human beings. Few are immune to its gaping jaws; so many of us seem to have an allergic reaction to being judged. And yet we continually judge ourselves and others.

The following question was recently posed during an online webinar: "What do you do when others are judging you?" This response was offered by my teacher, Valda Monroe:

"It is just you and God. There is no one else."

These words hit me hard and deep. And continue to do so. As we (and that certainly includes me) see deeper and yet deeper into their truth, we may find ourselves on the road to freedom from the vice-like grip of the chains of judgement.

We know other people have views. And we know that these opinions are their thoughts and perceptions, appearing true to them. Yet we also understand that these views are not *the* truth. Because by now we have realised that human beings can decide their own personal truths. We may find this difficult to accept but it is a pre-existing fact, whether we like it or not. The world was designed to include the personal views of all people. You cannot get away from that.

Judgement is a collective mass of thinking that looks true to someone. Yet somehow, when we feel judged, it feels like being punched in the stomach, or worse, stabbed in the back. Judgement certainly doesn't feel like another's passing energy merely spraying us with inconsequential residue. More often than not, it feels like a huge truck dumping wet cement on our living room floor.

The funny thing is that we are not consistent. We usually have a category of special people we cannot handle being judged by (mothers-in-law, anyone?); and another category who look harmless, naive or even helpful when they judge us. We give them a free pass. We do this on the basis of some reasoning that appears logical to us.

The other curious thing is that we can get high and mighty about being judged, waxing lyrical about those "awful judgmental villains". But as soon as we feel victimised by others, we so often begin to judge right back! Our egos go into protective overdrive, as if there is a holy war being waged that needs fighting. Weapons are prepared and sharpened repeatedly in our minds, weapons of resentment, hurt, betrayal, anger, insecurity – even retaliation. Our minds keep on attacking the "judgement enemy" with this arsenal of our own hurt and incensed thinking. And yet, still, the holy war escalates.

So here is what I have seen deeper this past year, during my own sometimes painful moments of feeling judged:

I cannot experience the outside world directly. Ever. It's me and it's God – the source of all physical, mental and spiritual life. Nothing else. At least there is nothing else available to me psychologically. So in truth, I cannot feel judged by another. It is not possible.

The Principles underpinning the human experience show us that all we ever experience or feel is Thought in the moment. So when we hear or feel or sense someone judging us, we are only hearing or feeling our thoughts of another's judgement. That's it. Full stop.

We are in a constant relationship with Thought. And all our relationships are made up of our thinking about others. So all we can ever experience is our thinking about another. About their goodness, about their not-so-goodness, about their judgement, about their praise. We think we are experiencing others' traits. But we are not. We are experiencing Thought.

This is the genius of the resilience with which we have all been gifted. It has an inbuilt design mechanism: if we feel judged, we are thinking judged. So if we think something like: "I guess I am not their favourite person"; or "wow, they are upset with me"; or "fancy that, they think I am a bit of a train wreck", we will feel that thinking.

I know now, after knocking my head against my own brick wall of judgment a few times this past year that it is possible to see past the illusion that tricks us into assuming that judgment is something that happens to us. I also know that feeling judged and judging others go hand in hand. So it's always good to look inwards at ourselves honestly. Not in judgement. But as a way to move forward.

Each time I bump up against this truth, it opens me up to a space beyond judgment where its illusion is revealed. This is a place of deeper connection to our souls. There is no feeling there of being judged.

There is us and there is God. Which is good news, because we are protected by the grace of a perfectly designed "God paradigm". Within its logic and wisdom, there is deeper understanding. And often, to our surprise, we fall headfirst into love and compassion.

BLOGSIGHT: *The outside-in illusion falsely assumes that judgement is something that happens to us. But when we hear or sense someone judging us, we are only feeling our thoughts of another's judgement. As we can only ever experience our own insecure and hurt feelings, it is actually not possible to feel judged by another.*

The "Weight" of Decision-Making – Not As Heavy As It Seems

Sam is a dedicated mother trying, like so many of us, to make the "right" decisions for her family. During the course of a recent session, she brought up how she was facing what she regarded as a big decision about where to take her children for their half-term holiday. The more obvious choice Sam was considering could potentially turn out to be a disaster, seeing that the other attendees were extended family members going through a particularly rough time. On the one hand, it seemed as if the wiser choice would be to avoid this option for her kids' sake. But on the other hand, Sam felt a sense of responsibility to be around these much-loved people in her life who would appreciate her support during this period. The decision appeared to be weighing heavily on her.

I asked Sam if she would be able to put this decision aside for a few days and promised we would come back to it towards the end of our time together. (We were in the midst of a four-day Intensive, which is an extended, individualised learning experience.) She agreed and I soon forgot about Sam's still-to-be-made decision. But then, at the end of the week, to her surprise, Sam announced that the decision had already been made. We didn't need to solve it.

What happened?

Without consciously thinking about it (which she had been doing incessantly for weeks on end until this point), Sam had arrived at a clear resolution: she wanted to spend the holiday with her extended family. The decision had made itself with minimal input from Sam, who found this strange, and commented it was probably just a fluke. To my mind, it wasn't a fluke at all.

Decision-making seems to plague many of us, barely giving respite from its suffocating intensity. Sam's experience got me thinking how the very people grappling with uncertainty and decision-making are often the same ones who seem to have a lot of decisions to make. Is this God having a sense of humour? "You guys are really bad at making decisions, so I will give you tons of decisions to struggle with!" Let's assume not.

So I am going to suggest this as a simple fact: we create our own reality.

There is a continuous flow of Thought that moves through our minds and guides us through life moment to moment. It is designed to seamlessly decide for us in a way that is so effortless and natural that we forget it is happening. This thinking does its job so well that it seems to manoeuvre us through our experiences, contemplating and discerning for us in a very simple, non-confrontational way.

When we get confused and bogged down with decisions, it is simply because we are considering factors that become false barriers to the natural flow of Thought. We are now factoring in what we refer to as "pros" and "cons". We feel this process is productive, responsible and necessary. But perhaps we need to take another look.

"Pros" (the implications of my decision that look as if they will create positive results and be "good" for me and my loved ones) and "cons" (the implications of my decision that look as if they may create negative results and thus potential harm for me or my loved ones) are rooted in a misunderstanding that is hard to see when it is playing loudly in the content of our minds. And so, our minds inevitably fill up with these distracting but seemingly important considerations.

Nothing outside of Thought in the moment can cause us to feel or experience anything in a psychological sense. These feelings are the sole domain of Thought. Knowing this, our understanding is now aligned with reality. Unburdened by the false assumption of how this reality is created, we are free to independently make decisions by virtue of what occurs in our thinking minds, moment to moment. Seeing this one truth will release us from the grip of our thinking that is preoccupied with weighing up the pros and cons.

I used to believe that making decisions (especially what looked to me to be the really important ones) carried huge weight and pressure. The "wrong" decision could potentially damage me or my children, my finances or my future in a life-changing kind of way.

Now, I can hear you shouting at the page: "But there *are* some life-altering decisions!"

Well, here's what I have come to realise. No matter what decisions I make, including the full consequences that they carry – and yes, I can and do make mistakes – the fact remains that my emotional well-being does not lie in my decisions or my mistakes. Of course, like most responsible adults, I try my best to be considered in my decision-making. But the fact that I might make a "wrong decision" does not figure highly in my mind.

Why? Because a wrong decision implies that we can decide something that will harm or limit us psychologically. This is not possible according to the logic of the inside-out understanding. And because of this logic, our minds free up to guide us in the direction of the most obvious next step.

I believe this is what happened to Sam. As this logic took root over the course of the week, the weight of her decision and its consequences receded. Sam was thus able to arrive painlessly and straightforwardly at an important decision, her concerns about getting it "right" or "wrong" temporarily suspended. This allowed the natural working of her mind to take over and get the job done. So it was no fluke at all!

It is worth getting curious and looking around at those members of the human race who seem to have been blessed with not having many decisions to make. Are they just blessed?

Or are they wiser to the blessings of the Mind?

BLOGSIGHT: *According to the inside-out logic, we cannot decide something that will harm us psychologically. As this understanding becomes more obvious to us, the presumed "weight" of decision-making recedes. Arriving at decisions can then become simpler and more straight-forward.*

Losing My Love of Football – The Endless Range of Thought

At the recent Three Principles Global Conference in Los Angeles, Eirik Golsen spoke about working with a single client. He called this client: "The World". Eirik observed that we don't really know much about the world – outside of our own thinking about it. The only world we know is the world of our minds. So to really help this "client", we need to begin to listen to the world. I loved that.

Eirik's words resonated strongly for me because their message is so humbling. We think we see things as they really are. And then we surprise ourselves when others do not see them as we do, or when we have a change of heart or mind and our view changes.

However, when we understand that we are always peering into life via the constant power of Thought, we realise how temporary and transient, how malleable and fragile, our image of reality really is. It is built on Thought – and thus can collapse in an instant.

I experienced one such "thought collapse" right after the London Olympics in the summer of 2012.

But first, here's a slightly embarrassing disclaimer that really threw me.

I grew up sports-mad. This was fairly common in South Africa in the early 1980s, even for a young girl. Our domestic football was pretty disinteresting to me at the time, but there were two English football clubs that most South Africans supported. It was either Liverpool or Manchester United. Luckily for me, my family were Man U fans. (Now, you Liverpool fans – behave and don't throw this book at anyone!)

When I married Brian, having only dated for five weeks, it occurred to me that I had ignorantly forgotten to find out which club he supported (I must have really been infatuated). Thank goodness he was also an ardent Man U fan. Phew! The stars were clearly aligned. And to emphasise the point, life took a perfect turn when, not long after we came to live in the UK, Brian's surprise anniversary gift to me was a trip to Old Trafford – the brilliantly named "Theatre of Dreams" – to watch our team thrash Spurs. It was a magical moment. Long live the beautiful game!

But here comes the really interesting part. Years later, when the Olympic Games finally came to London, I was struck by the relative humility and unpretentiousness of the London Olympians, which was in sharp contrast to the excess and apparent arrogance of so many of our top footballers. Many of these understated Olympic athletes were unknown to us, especially the handball players, kayakers and skeet shooters (what is skeet shooting anyway?). But they seemed genuinely hardworking, unassuming and, for the most part, pretty down to earth.

Suddenly, much to my horror, I developed an aversion to footballers. I became highly judgemental of anyone over the age of sixteen running around a rectangular patch of grass in long socks trying to manoeuvre a round ball into a net held up by two vertical posts connected to a horizontal bar. (This caused some unexpected problems in my marriage, as this is the very activity Brian engages in most Sunday mornings.) I couldn't help it. I simply could not bear to watch or listen to anything football related. My love of football died with one swift stroke of the sword.

Unwilling to just roll over without a fight, I tried to rediscover my passion. But despite my efforts, I was unable to find relief from what had suddenly become very boring and dull. (This really surprised me as football had never been boring before – even a nil-nil draw.) But so it was. I had to surrender to my new reality.

It has been four years since that epic "thought collapse". And yes, the universe has been good to me, as Manchester United is no longer the team they were during Sir Alex's reign; the Theatre of Dreams has lost some of its lustre.

A similar experience has threatened to happen in the past with chocolate. It's just that I have decided to draw the line here: I categorically refuse to *not* be a chocolate addict. So even though I do not enjoy chocolate that much anymore, I still eat copious amounts of it! Go figure.

We all live in a constant world of Thought. This is instantly brought to life in a way that appears as if our thinking will be this way forever. What we experience in each moment seems entrenched and true, for all time.

But I have come to appreciate that although the power of Thought is constant, we experience it moment to moment. The feelings I had believed football was giving me – joy, exhilaration, heartbreak – were actually being created from my thinking about the so-called beautiful game. So it makes perfect sense that when my thinking changed, the feelings changed. New thinking emerged. I didn't do anything. It was done for me. This is how the Mind operates.

And it is guaranteed that this will consistently happen. There will always be a subtraction of thinking. So we will be gloriously, consistently inconsistent.

Knowing that a "thought collapse" is possible, even when we least expect it, is something to be celebrated. Even if it means we lose our love of football.

But chocolate is where I draw the line!

BLOGSIGHT: *We all live in a constant world of Thought. As Thought is moment to moment, it is absolutely predictable that we will experience a change of mind. We all have the potential to experience a "Thought collapse".*

Separate Realities

A powerful implication of the inside-out logic of the mind is the idea of separate realities. Valda Monroe and Keith Blevens brilliantly lay out the truth of this implication, which I have summarised as follows:

When we recognise that our minds only operate from the inside-out, we do not waste time being dismayed that others do not think like us. We understand that one person actually cannot have another person's thoughts and that no one can think the same as anyone else. As much as I may think it would be better if you would think like me, it cannot happen. This puts us in a position to respect differences of opinion, and enables us to listen and communicate better.

When we mistakenly believe that our minds operate from the outside-in, separate realities are not obvious to us. When others do not think like us we wonder if there is something wrong. We stay trapped in the illusion that others should be thinking the same, stirring up unnecessary and often unhelpful reactions.

Last week I sat in the car in our driveway as one of my sons explained how he had reached a dead end: he couldn't find a resolution between himself and his school. He felt that he had honestly and thoroughly looked into his own mind, and concluded that despite his best efforts he could not extend himself any more in terms of what the school expected of him.

The school had a different view, of course. As its leadership seemed unwilling to shift from that view, the message to my son was pretty much along the lines of, "Our way or the highway!"

He didn't regard this as unfair. He's had a lifetime of learning from Brian and me that we are not "victims of unfair". In his mature and balanced view, he understood that the school would not budge in what they were demanding. He wasn't angry about it. He was just at a loss what to do.

It's a curious thing how we superficially form opinions about people and arrive at conclusions. We don't look deeper than what meets our eye, which is usually just beyond our peripheral vision. Yet I have learned that there is always a solution that lies outside of what we can see. Insight is available in every moment. And so I was hopeful that one might emerge, even though I had absolutely no inkling of it in my line of sight or thought.

My son asked if I could help by coming with him to talk to his head teacher. I said that I would. I presumed I understood his side of things and felt I also understood the school's side. Then he said, "Mom, I know you think you understand me. But you don't."

For the briefest of moments, I felt myself becoming defensive. *I do get where he is coming from*, I thought to myself. But a split second later, I came away from this line of thinking. What I know about separate realities told me that he was factually correct. We can never fully immerse into someone else's world of Thought.

So I turned to him and asked, "Why don't you tell me more about what you are feeling? I *want* to understand better."

He then let me in a little further into his internal world – and I stepped in a little more deeply. I felt so connected to him. It was a moment of seeing into his heart, his soul. I was so full of love and compassion. It was such a special experience: however much I thought I got this child, I saw that there was much more. It humbled me and gave me so much respect for him and his reality.

The next day we had the meeting at the school that potentially carried significant implications for my son's future education in the school. (And not in a good way!) My son and I had reasonable insight into the head teacher's view and were respectful of it. We just didn't know how to close the chasm between the two positions. It felt like the Grand Canyon lay between them.

So what was the result? Did a solution emerge?

Well, you may be disappointed to hear that a solution has not yet materialised. We failed to bridge the gap between our respective thinking. And the situation has not really improved since then.

But here's the thing: from my perspective, the meeting at the school was a very generative dialogue. There was no arguing or defending of positions. I was so proud of my son. He showed maturity and was respectful and insightful. I also saw how he had been constantly learning from the situation. Although I obviously do not wish to see him struggle, I am grateful that he has had an opportunity to learn that his thinking and another person's thinking does not have to be the same. In truth, it can never be the same. I love that he gets to see that just because we don't agree with another's point of view does not necessarily invalidate it or us. And I love that we can have a connecting, informative dialogue with no obvious resolution, which still provides a meaningful learning opportunity.

I am not sure how this will play out or where we will end up. But I trust both my son and myself that we will do the best we can with the thinking that occurs and makes sense to us, moment to moment.

In the meantime, we have become closer, my son and I. And we are both enjoying a deeper appreciation of the endless depth of separate realities.

BLOGSIGHT: Separate realities are an implication of the inside-out logic of how we create our psychological experience. When we recognise that our minds only operate one way, we are not dismayed that others do not think like us. As much as we may prefer for others to think like us, it simply cannot happen. Contained within this one truth is a built-in direction towards resolution.

We All Inhale the Same Psychological Oxygen

Brian and I recently had the opportunity to speak to a group of people we had never met before. They were attending a week-long employability course, designed to convey the skills required to write a CV, prepare for an interview and to generally re-enter the job-searching market. We had only one short hour, mid-course, to speak with the participants, who knew nothing about us or what we teach. We began by telling them that we were there to discuss the human dimension – the invisible piece in their quest to get back into work life. Actually, in our opinion, the essential piece we all need for life – job or no job.

And boy, were they hungry for it!

I was touched by the reaction of our audience when I shared with them how the doubts and fears they expressed, when sitting across from their interviewer, are actually the same feelings felt by their would-be employer. Everyone around the employment "table" is a human being, replete with their own goals and aspirations. Hearts that beat the same way, blood that runs through veins according to the same process. People who share doubts, insecurities, worries, hopes and dreams for the future.

I could tell that this was news to those attending the training, and that they felt somewhat different and alienated. Their world was divided into those who have and those who don't have. Those who are smart and those who are not. Those who suffer and those who prosper. Those who struggle and those who "have their stuff together". What a common and significant misunderstanding.

Yet I empathised, for I knew where this misunderstanding came from. I too used to think I was different and alienated. Sometimes I still have those lonely, isolating moments when I feel as if life is turning on its axis and I am standing stationary on my own separate, small island.

I realise now that this is not possible. We are all bound together, connected psychologically as well as spiritually. Some think it is just the spiritual part that we are all connected to. But you cannot separate one from the other. The Mind informs both. It is the life-force of both.

When we realise the invisible thread that runs through *all* our mental lives, we grasp that we are all of one deeper Mind, one deeper Thought and one deeper Consciousness. Just as physiologically we breathe from the same oxygen, so too psychologically do we inhale the same pure oxygen. The oxygen of the Mind is pure, creative intelligence. This explains the incredible achievements of the world in which we live. This is the exquisite power of Thought.

And then there is free will. This is when we get to exhale. And we exhale whatever our understanding of life is. There is absolute freedom with our exhale, which is where the confusion and the insecurity of the world are formed.

Many of the people who come to learn with us believe they are the only ones going through issues, oftentimes feeling crippled by pressure and social concerns. Their problems seem weighty and complex. It is as if they are attempting to analyse every breath they take (to paraphrase the classic Police song) and "get it right".

But they have simply forgotten that they have been breathing since they entered the world. The universal resource of the Mind is providing them with infinite oxygen. They think and experience just like they breathe. Until they leave this world, they will never run out of the oxygen of ideas, creativity and solutions as they join the rest of humanity in "figuring life out".

They, like all human beings, have merely fallen out of rhythm with their own breath. They attribute their pain and confusion – their feelings – to other factors. This alienates them from the breath. The breath of the Mind – Thought – is what brings us all back to ourselves. It is this breath that is the very energy keeping us alive and connecting us to the heartbeat of the universe.

Reminding ourselves and those we meet that we are all of one breath and one spirit is not only hopeful, it is also true. To recognise that our problems and fears; our hopes and dreams are all of one creation and therefore we are always bound together shows us that your worries are my worries and your fears are my fears. Your hopes are my hopes and your dreams are my dreams.

Perhaps not in the finer details but certainly in the fabric that makes us all human, as we do our best inhaling and exhaling God's breath.

BLOGSIGHT: *When we realise the invisible thread that runs through all mental life, we see that we all inhale the same pure oxygen psychologically. We are connected by virtue of the universal Principles of Mind, Consciousness and Thought.*

Life – A Tale of Hope and Healing

During a recent eleven-hour flight en route to the One Solution Conference in Cape Town, I was transfixed by a moving and heart-warming documentary called *Life*. *Life* tells the story of Owen Suskind who is a lively, talkative and outgoing boy until he is diagnosed with severe autism at the age of three. Owen suddenly withdraws into a silent world, not uttering a single comprehensible word for the next four years.

Then, shortly before his seventh birthday, something astonishing occurs. Out of the blue, Owen remarks to his older brother, Walter, who was feeling sad on his birthday, "Walter doesn't want to grow up, just like Mowgli or Peter Pan." This was a remarkably perceptive insight for any child, let alone one with apparently severe cognitive limitations. And so began a new way for Owen to communicate with the world and engage with the people in his life. The ensuing inspirational story is a powerful testament to the intelligence and wisdom that operates within all of us no matter how dire and hopeless the situation appears.

Walt Disney films became Owen's keyhole to reconnecting with the outside world. Not only did he rediscover language and empathy through the animated movies, but the films also gave Owen a sense of purpose and belonging because of his deep identification with the "sidekick" characters. (These are characters generally regarded as subordinate to the main character they accompany. Think Donkey for Shrek or Tonto for The Lone Ranger.)

Owen owns a copy of every Disney film ever made; he knows each one of them virtually by heart. By design, Walt Disney characters over-express their emotions and facial expressions. This helped Owen understand them in a way that is far less obscure than trying to read human facial expressions. Ironic as it sounds, Disney characters leave nothing to the imagination. They bring feelings of love, loss, joy, rejection, fear, hope and the full range of the emotional spectrum to the surface.

The documentary depicts Owen immersed in watching Dumbo, the famous flying elephant of the 1940's cartoon film, as he leaves his family home on the eve of Owen's own transition to independent living. He, like Dumbo, grasps that he has the capacity to make this shift, depart the family nest and find his wings. We see Owen watch Bambi suffer the loss of his mother to cruel hunters as he spends his first night alone in his own flat without his mother to take care of him. We observe how the documentary's central protagonist takes in the words of the Little Mermaid's crab Sebastian, before graduating from Riverview School. "Well, it's like I always say, your Majesty, children got to be free to live their own lives."

Owen identifies with the sidekicks in the films he watches, resonating with their position as not quite the main character, often pushed aside for their differences. Yet the sidekicks become a source of great insight for Owen. His mind, via the power of Thought, finds peace within, knowing that those on the so-called "sidelines" are integral to the bigger story. There is always more than meets the eye.

The past does not exist as a barrier to our present. We are truly only experiencing Thought in each moment. And contained in each moment is a microcosm of potential that is infinite and unknown.

This is what Owen's story brings to life. Thus, it should be no surprise to us that Owen's first words after such a long hiatus of communication were not "mommy" or "daddy", rather a complex sentence replete with deep insight into his brother's emotional world.

With the steadfast support of his loving and hopeful family, Owen makes great progress. He demonstrates remarkable insight into his own emotional world and understands the limitations of how he appears in the eyes of others.

I subsequently read a couple of film reviews that asserted that even the magic of Disney could not prepare Owen for his disappointments and the nuances of life's day-to-day challenges. But I saw Owen react exactly as I or any other person would to these challenges. He experienced fear when in the misunderstanding that the unknown is scary. He was devastated when he thought love could only be experienced within a particular relationship, and that the end of that relationship signalled the end of love. He was anxious when preparing to write a speech to be delivered in front of a large audience (I can relate to this one!). And he felt off balance by not knowing what others wanted from him.

These common "life" scenarios might have looked more pronounced when experienced by Owen. But they are all a part of human living. When we mistakenly feel at the effect of our circumstances, we often seem to momentarily lose our way. We get frightened and feel lost and hopeless.

Owen is no different to me and you in that way. And like me and you, Owen finds his way again and again. He is deeply insightful. He is deeply connected. He sees from within. He finds, via Disney as a medium, a way to connect to the outside world. His mind uncovers an incredibly intelligent way – so incredible that documentary footage is required to make it believable – to pave the pathway for communication and relationships. Owen's journey through life is so different – and yet so familiar. This profound message is perfectly captured towards the documentary's denouement when Owen's father poignantly asks, "Who gets to say what a meaningful life is?"

It is deeply reassuring to realise how we are all finding our way, tripping over our own psychological misunderstandings and being picked up by our own in the moment insight as she straightens us up and dusts us off. No one is immune from the ongoing learning that is our lives.

This is a tale of resilience: a resilient boy, growing into a resilient man, creating a network of resilient autistic friends with a resilient family in the background and foreground.

There is great hope and healing in Owen's remarkable story. We would all do well to bear this in mind and to recall the profound words with which my friend and colleague, Dr Bill Petit, concluded his address at the One Solution Conference:

"A diagnosis is where you are, not *who* you are!"

BLOGSIGHT: *No one is immune to moments when we mistakenly assume ourselves to be at the effect of our circumstances, leaving us feeling frightened and even hopeless. But each time we remember the real source of our experience, we occupy the domain of the infinite wisdom perfectly contained in each moment of life.*

Me Before You – Our Human Story

I recently watched the film *Me Before You* and it had me in a flood of tears. I know I was not alone in creating a mini swimming pool around my seat as it tugged at my heartstrings. In fact, you would probably be alone if you were the dry-eyed person in the room! The movie highlighted many themes that speak to the very heart and soul of what it means to be human and live a meaningful life. Below is a short summary (spoiler alert!) for those who don't know the plot of the bestselling book by Jo Moyes, upon which the film's adapted screenplay was based.

The story begins with a glimpse into the life of a wealthy, successful, good-looking (such are the movies, after all!), fun-loving young man, Will. Will has the perfect existence – in his mind – until the moment he gets hit by a motorcycle while crossing the street, instantly becoming quadriplegic.

Louisa, a warm, open, quirky and compassionate young woman from the "wrong side of the tracks", answers an advertisement on a whim and is subsequently employed to care for Will against his wishes. (All the other "professional" carers did not get past the interview stage with Will.) Impervious to his initial rudeness and cynicism, Louisa sticks with Will and over time, manages to restore some of his spirit, zest for life and sense of humour.

Unsurprisingly, they soon fall in love with each other. However, the immense anger and depression Will feels as a result of being imprisoned in his own body always simmers beneath the surface. In spite of Louisa's support and love, Will simply cannot come to terms with his new reality and the life he has lost. Before meeting Louisa he had already decided to end his life via assisted suicide, though he had promised to give his devoted parents six months before going through with that fateful decision. They hoped he would change his mind, a hope that gathers steam when Louisa enters his life and heart.

It is striking to see the separate realities being played out in the film.

Will's mother cannot accept his decision. Will is her son and whatever form he now lives in, he is still her son. No more, no less. And her love for him is no more, no less. It is an incredibly powerful representation of the limitless and unconstrained love we all have within us. I recognise this love within me. It sits at the very core of who we are, penetrating right through any beliefs, thoughts, expectations and conditions we create.

Will's father also loves his son deeply, but somehow seems to be able to come to terms with his belief that this is his son's decision to make. This allows his father some distance from the reality of the unspeakable loss that faces them.

Louisa is remarkably resolute in her belief that she can show Will how much beauty, love, fun, lightness and joy is still available to him in spite of his permanent physical incapacitation. She sees beyond Will's external condition, and is convinced that this will penetrate his soul, awakening within him a deep desire to be in life no matter what. For Louisa, joy and love are unconditional and not tied to circumstance.

And yet, despite Louisa's love for Will and love for life, he cannot and does not accept his new reality. Towards the end of film, Will emphatically tells her, "This is not my life." He lovingly explains to Louisa that though she has awakened in him more happiness and joy, it is *still* not his life and nothing will change that. Ever. It is heart-breaking and deeply moving to see that she cannot change his mind. No one can change Will's mind.

And as for me, I was surprised and moved to discover that despite having my own opinion on Will's decision, my view temporarily flew out of the window as I generated a slither of understanding into his inner world.

I felt my own judgement fall away as I met Will for a split second – in *his* mind, not my mind. There arose compassion in place of judgement or frustration.

I joined the rest of the audience in being granted a glimpse into the usually invisible threads of thought that forms a person's behaviours and decisions.

Me Before You **is a beautiful illustration of how each of us operates from our own mind, but are threaded and tied together through the power of love and connection. This makes us all know what it means to feel hopelessness, despair and a sense of being lost, while at the same time feel connected to love, beauty and life. This is what it means to be part of a Universal Mind.**

The film's ending was incredibly sad but somehow uplifting. Will left a unique legacy to Louisa in the form of a beautifully crafted letter. He asked of her to live and love fully and wholly – and not limit herself with this gift of life she had. Yet the sadness was that he did not grasp that he could have had the same opportunity.

Will did not see his gift. And because he didn't see it, it didn't exist. For what we see is what we live. We know no other life than the one that is created in our minds eye.

Yes, I wanted Will to live. *I* felt the possibility that he did not feel. I could touch it. I could smell it. But he could not.

By the end of the film, there was no room for my personal judgement or opinion. Only a reservoir of compassion and love for the human story we are all doing our best to live in. I hope and pray that this will inspire me to be a little more loving and a little less judging, even when I cannot see into the minds and hearts of others.

BLOGSIGHT: *Separate realities means that we all operate and experience life through our own thinking minds. However, we are all tied together through the power of love and connection.*

Is Love the Weak and Passive Option?

It was fascinating to observe the wide range of reactions to the news of the unexpected (for many) victory of the new president elect of America, Donald Trump. For many of those who had not supported Trump, there was an almost existential need to make sense of things and consider how to look forward. Some proposed "love" as being the only answer, implying that the election result needed to be met with a kind of benevolent equanimity (my made-up phrase). This angered others, who believed that "action" was required, implying the necessity to take a more proactive, assertive stand. These widely differing perspectives led me to reflect on some of the greatest change-makers the world has known.

Curiously, many of the most influential leaders in history seemed to have such an immense impact when they acted out of love. Martin Luther King, Ghandi and Mandela were all known to have initially treaded a path of aggression and belligerent resistance. Once these inspirational trailblazers began pursuing a more loving and peaceful direction, they were able to experience an exponential leap in making a difference that defied and eventually transformed commonly accepted thought at the time. History shows that there was nothing passive about these remarkable human beings who changed the world in which they lived.

In the following condensed extract from a fascinating article written by Danica Apolline entitled *Love is Freedom*, the author describes the very divergent paths taken by Nelson and Winnie Mandela in response to the suffering they endured and witnessed. (Note that omissions and minor editorial changes are mine.)

The film "Mandela" triggered in me a powerful reflection of where we are at in the evolution of our planet. I was first inspired by Nelson Mandela as a teenager, watching him leave twenty-seven years in prison a peaceful man, and shortly afterwards reading his autobiography, "Long Walk to Freedom".

Yet there was something – or someone – I had not given the attention that was also deserved, and who really stood out for me whilst I watched the film. Winnie Mandela. Nelson's second wife, a determined, powerful woman who many in South Africa looked up to. She is called "Mamu Winnie" by many – Mother Winnie. Watching her story unfold through the film, I was inspired to think about our greatest power.

Winnie Mandela was a strong, intelligent, bright woman who spent sixteen months in solitary confinement in a cockroach infested concrete box of a cell, during Nelson's imprisonment. She was beaten, assaulted and abused by the prison officers – in addition to all that she experienced, living with two small children and no income at times, separated from the husband she adored, regularly harassed by the apartheid police. She reacted... as a woman battered by the Apartheid regime – and what that did to her.

Winnie Mandela turned to hate. She was so angry and bitter about all she lost, and as a leader in the ANC, resorted to championing the "fight". She authorised the brutal executions of informants, and became militarised. She wanted others to hurt as she was hurting. She wanted to cause others the pain she felt. She represented the anger and rage of the oppressed black population, and they looked to her as someone who understood them. In that rage, South Africa was on the brink of civil war, until Nelson Mandela – bringing a message of peace, equality and reconciliation – changed that. Mandela himself said that "the only victory they ever had over me was what they did to her."

So how does seeing this help us understand our greatest power?

I was reminded, watching "Mandela", that both Winnie and Nelson suffered hugely at the hands of the Apartheid regime. But that each chose a different response. Mandela, for all his imprisonment, knew that the only way to true freedom was to forgive and to let his anger go. He realised that choosing peace was the only way to freedom. Mandela showed us that our greatest power is the power of choice.

We are living in a time where there is so much that can make us angry. I meet healers and therapists who would rather be angry about the behaviour of large corporations, or the problems of capitalism. If we choose to build a world based on love, then we must first choose to be loving – and that means to all those who we perceive might be causing us a challenge in our lives.

That is what seeing "Mandela" reminded me of this weekend. Being in your freedom is an expression of your power to create the world you choose, as Nelson taught us.

I found Apolline's article very insightful. But it is important to further flesh out what, according to my understanding, lay at the core of Nelson Mandela's ability to choose differently from Winnie. Having read numerous books about his life, I believe that the key to Mandela's deep insight about how to create change was an understanding of separate realities.

He grasped that because we all see life through our own thinking minds, no one can truly understand the hearts and minds of another.

This led him, during his final years in prison, to really listen to his oppressors; to try for the first time to understand the thoughts and feelings that gave birth to their ideology. In so doing, Mandela saw beyond the fear and hatred to the very genuine humanity of his own jailers. Once he insightfully understood how human beings work, this was the only option that made sense to this remarkable man. It was an act of immense greatness and humility – and a deep understanding regarding how we create our realities.

When Mandela realised this universal truth of separate realities, it seems to me that the peaceful and loving path was no longer a choice. It became the way. The only way.

It is an error to assume that the path of love is weak or passive. Frustration, fear and anger are *not* necessary requirements for action, change, transformation, innovation, creation and even revolution. This is part of Nelson Mandela's legacy to us.

Here's a thought: the least passive act in history was the creation of the universe. And there is no doubt in my mind that it was a divine act born of love – not anger.

> BLOGSIGHT: *An implication of seeing how we all live in separate realities is a world of deeper wisdom, love, compassion and respect for others. Conversely, an implication of not recognising separate realities is a world of insecure and fearful feelings leading to self-justification, aggression and greater conflict.*

When Life Throws You a Few "Curveballs"

Definition of a curveball (mine): *Events that do not cooperate with my preference or expectation.*

I had it all figured out. In my mind's eye, I was going to take a well-deserved break from work, domestic responsibilities, laundry, London traffic and blog writing: a long-awaited two-week holiday in South Africa, reconnecting with family, friends and the raw African beauty of my childhood.

I have seen others make similar predictions and indeed return from holiday inspired, enthused, relaxed and recharged. So I assumed this to be a reasonable expectation for myself. Well, as I often teach – but still frequently forget – life dances to its own tune. Another way of saying this is that when we think about the future, we have an incomplete equation. This time, while I was dancing merrily away, life somehow "forgot" to take my thoughts and desires into account once again.

There were quite a few unexpected challenges that showed up over the period of our vacation.

The very sudden and shocking passing of an extremely close relative in the middle of our time away was by far the saddest. Our hearts and plans were thrown into turmoil; we needed to adjust emotionally as well as take into account the practicalities of losing a loved one halfway across the world.

There were other "curveballs" that came our way, the specific details of which are not really the point. But what is the point, as always, are the learning opportunities that were showed up for me.

For the first time in a long while, I found myself waking up with a jolt at five in the morning to an avalanche of thoughts and feelings. I felt buried beneath the feeling of insecurity and doubt. My much-anticipated break from life had turned into an inescapable storm of thinking. The weather outside was perfect for a holiday. But inside my mind, it wouldn't stop raining.

My dark thoughts were accompanied by that old, though still familiar feeling of dread, coursing through my sensory system, as if I was free-falling off a cliff. I was. The illusionary cliff of my own thinking.

I was curious as to why it was taking so long for my mind to settle. But hey, impatience is made up of thought too, so what can a girl do?

Here's the really interesting part, the part that makes sense when we realise that our experience of life comes alive only through our thinking in the moment. In the gaps between the dark moments, I was able to relax and be present. While the sun set over the mountains, I went horse riding on what is surely one of the most beautiful stretches of beach in the world. It was heaven. I met 500-pound sea lions; went bike-riding with my husband and son along the magnificent coastal promenade; ran for miles against an exquisite backdrop too beautiful to capture with the written word. I laughed, cried, shared, reminisced and connected with old friends and family. Slowly, I felt myself moving forward. As my mind gradually settled down, there was a falling away of the need to resist the "curveballs" life had sent my way.

There is nothing from the outside that can harm us; there is nothing from the outside that can help us. So curveballs cannot harm us – but we sure can be fooled into thinking they can.

The infinite power of the Mind engenders immense awe and respect. There are no limits to what it can create. As human beings, we have the capacity to think. This extraordinary gift has been our greatest blessing, and at times, when we lose sight of this gift, our greatest "curse".

Throughout time, human beings have created rich and diverse chapters of history through their thinking minds. This creative intelligence has been the catalyst, via the power of Thought, for all the love stories and all the conflicts. Through its power we have birthed the greatest peace treaties and initiated the most senseless wars. We have has composed the most tender love songs and the most heart-wrenching poems. We have discovered new frontiers in the sciences and arts. We have uncovered new planets and solar systems. We have feared and forgiven. We have criticised and praised. We have created paranoia and resentment. We have grieved and healed. We have fantasised and imagined. We have remembered and forgotten. There is no moment in life that has not originated from its very bosom.

We are a part of a spiritual Mind that is beyond anything that the greatest human mind can engineer. Not even a creative genius like Mark Zuckerberg will ever be able to create the potential that he and all of us have to love, inspire, suffer, heal, misunderstand and understand. The power to learn and the power to generate insight. The creative power of the Mind is an all-encompassing free gift through which we experience everything – the totality of all of life.

When it feels as if life does not fall in line with my expectations – what I call my "curveballs" – this is not in and of itself a problem. Expectations are not problematic even if they are not met. They only become a problem when I forget the Thought-feeling connection. But when I *do* have an awareness of this connection, I have an opportunity to get on board with what it is, instead of judging it. This offers a chance for evolution. It throws me back into reality, back into the present moment.

And I am more than equipped to be here.

BLOGSIGHT: *As free thinkers we get to think and feel independently of whatever curveballs we may come up against. Knowing this one spiritual and psychological fact emboldens us when facing events that do not cooperate with our preferences or expectations.*

Beyond What to Do and How to Do It

The blind spot concerns not the what and how they do it – but the who: who we are, and the inner place or source from which we operate, both individually and collectively.

—Otto Scharmer, *Presence*

"Tell me what to do and how to do it" is one of the most common requests of the many students and clients interested in learning about the Principles of Innate Health. And they are very sincere. They want to learn. They want to escape the stress and pain of living in a world that often feels overwhelming and hostile, or frustrating and confusing. The locus of power they have given to the outside world creates an illusory vice from which they want to break free.

I can relate. When lost in the outside-in misunderstanding, the fragmentation of my analytical mind gains momentum. Then, like everyone else, I feel compelled to find the answers to fixing, improving and changing my inner and outer worlds. But I have come to appreciate that relentlessly seeking answers to the whats and the hows is a bit like a small child forever chasing the elusive butterfly. It is a mirage.

Every time I get a glimpse of the whole, the bigger picture, or what I think of as the "oneness of life", these questions become redundant. When I fall into the truth that exists beyond the fragmentation and separation, the potential exists for life to unfold far more effortlessly. This is where unification is found. When we become aligned to how we work psychologically, new knowledge is revealed that would otherwise not be accessible.

If you are not interested in a truth greater than your own personal one, this learning is likely to be frustrating. It addresses an unconditional, universal, pre-existing truth that has stood the test of time. It has travelled through the ages unscarred and unchanged. It is constant – the backdrop to every life story that plays out and unfolds on this earth and beyond.

It is a truth that encapsulates every human experience that ever was and ever will be. It holds the secret to all of life. It is freely offered as a gift to anyone and everyone. It comes from a place beyond the conditioned mind that reveals reality as it is, not as it appears to be.

This level of revelation holds nothing back. There are no half-truths here. But I can assure you, the insightful learning that this understanding brings is uplifting, filled with sweeter love and more profound wisdom than you ever dreamed possible.

Does this explanation of the human operating system disconnect us from everyday life? Of course not. It allows us to get our hands dirty and play the game of life as rough and tumble as it gets. No one is immune from the human condition.

Yet insightfully learning how our minds work opens the doorway to a deeper order than meets the eye. It has a profound logic and built-in wisdom. And through this doorway we will continually catch glimpses of the perfection and beauty of the whole as it manifests in the moment-to-moment tapestry of our lives with its inevitable ups and downs. This beauty goes beyond words and what comes from this deeper place will align our intellect with timeless knowledge.

And as for the other times? The moments when you feel trapped in the dark? Well, I consider the immutable inside-out logic of the Principles as the slither of light under the door. This illumination is your torch, your guide, your compass. It teaches us that all life, all moments, are created equal. The positive and the negative, the lightness and the darkness. It teaches us that the potential for insight is included in each moment. We can now rest in this knowledge.

So throw away the whats and the hows. They are now redundant. The single discriminator of how our psychological experience works and how it does not is life changing. It's profound, self-correcting logic will educate you, evolve you and provide you with an absolute direction back to truth.

> BLOGSIGHT: *Understanding how our minds really work is the gateway to gaining a glimpse of the whole. This is a deeper order of truth that reveals reality as it is, not as it appears to be.*

Afterword: The Learning of Being Human

I never set out to write a weekly blog. As a busy, working mother of six, I had other aspirations about how to spend my time on a Sunday evening. (Lying in bed sipping a Gin & Tonic while Brian preoccupied himself in the kitchen making homemade organic gnocchi for me, and fresh fruit-smoothies for the kids had always sounded more appealing!)

But if there was anything I learnt over the past 43 years, it is that life very rarely goes how you intend it to go. So in my role as director of the Innate Health Centre, whose mission is to explain the source of our innate mental well-being and resilience – and having grown tired of waiting for the gnocchi – I decided it was time to start sharing my reflections and insights in the form of a short weekly blog.

What began as a brief Monday morning message from the Innate Health Centre soon grew into a weekly snapshot of my own life: my struggles and triumphs, my ups and downs, my moments of joy and moments of misery. But these musings were far from random in terms of the underlying implication. No matter what was going on inside my head and heart at the time, underpinning these reflections was always one fundamental theme: the *inside-out logic of how we psychologically experience life.*

Most weeks, when I sat down on my bed or on the bike at the gym to write the week's blog I had absolutely no idea what to say. Seriously. So I would challenge myself to start tapping the touch keys on my iPhone and see what emerged. (Believe it or not, every one of the initial drafts was written entirely on my phone; perhaps a better book title would have been "Insights from an iPhone"?) Each week, out of this space of "nothingness", the Mind offered me in the moment insights that I had unknowingly been living with and learning during that past week. So to me, writing these weekly reflections has just been another illustration of the inherent human capacity for inevitable evolution, for sharper clarity, for awakening to deeper feelings and for understanding and truth to emerge.

Every essay has encapsulated a glimpse into the very ordinary, and yet paradoxically extraordinary business of human living. Much of the outline of my life has emerged over the course of these reflections – children, work, family, faith, relationships, holidays, expectations, disappointments, new opportunities – pretty much the entire gamut of day-to-day living.

From the mundanity of dealing with kids' bedtime to the surreal moments of deep connection when I was suddenly beset with a mysterious neurological illness. From the pain of hearing about a young girl's rejection to the sheer joy of horse riding with my four-year-old son in one of the most exquisite places on earth. From insights gleaned from peaches and coconuts, giraffes, illusionists, employment training, Walt Disney films, Manchester United and my own children to learning about judgement, decision-making, addictive thinking and dealing with exhaustion, hurt, pain, loss and disappointment. From the confusion generated by the election of a new president to the legacy of love and clarity left by some of the greatest leaders the world has known. From the deep insights that emerged in some of my darkest moments to the inspiration generated from the moving journey of a profoundly deaf friend. From the lessons that I have learned from children as young as eight, to the deep understanding that has emerged through learning from extraordinary and gifted teachers I am blessed to call friends and colleagues. From the moments I felt vulnerable, confused and deeply challenged, to the times I felt inspired, clear and full of hope.

They were all there, because they were all moments of learning for me.

The profound explanation that all experience only ever works one way re-engaged me with a love of learning. I had assumed that this kind of innate, in-the-moment, real-time learning was the sole domain of the under-fives' or those crazy but lucky adults who never seemed to properly grow up. But I had been wrong. Anytime I found myself comprehending and awake to the truth of how my experience was coming to life, it simultaneously revealed an appreciation for the fact that I and every human is already wired for learning. This truth revealed an absolute direction for continued insight and inevitable growth. It revealed the always reliable, single, true or false discriminator of whether I was being deceived by an innocent illusion or whether I was seeing through the facade. These essays are a testimonial of this natural unfolding. They are a window into my weekly learning.

And if the blogs are the window, there is one common frame on which it all rests: the Principles that are the one, singular and constant cause and catalyst of all human experience.

Waking up to these Principles undoubtedly forced change in my perspective and the direction of my life. Mostly in a way I did not expect. I thought, for a while, that an understanding of the human mind would enable me to live life in a state of equanimity and spiritual serenity. It would open me up to experiencing a constantly beautiful feeling, a deeply quiet mind and a consistent capacity to be non-reactive to the events of my life. That has not been the case, though I have certainly experienced and enjoyed more of the above at different times.

Mostly, this learning has brought about a peace with myself. An embrace of my humanity. And an embrace of the humanity of others – far more than I ever thought possible. A knowing that I too am susceptible to fall into misunderstanding and be carried into the ego of self-importance. And a knowing that emotional security and psychological safety are my birthright; a birthright that can never, ever be dependent on outside factors. It simply does not work this way.

And finally, but perhaps most important of all, this learning has allowed me to run into God on a daily basis in a way I never dreamt possible.

So I invite you to join me on the ongoing journey of learning. Who knows what or who you may run into on the way?

As I write the final words of this book, I am struck yet again how I find myself on a continuous learning journey that is constantly evolving. What you will read is only a reflection of my understanding up to this point; my best attempt to convey a pre-existing truth way beyond my own personal truth or current knowledge. No matter who you are and how long you have been immersed in this learning, we will all fall out of alignment with seeing the logic and truth of the Principles creating our reality. In this way we are all the same. There are no experts. We all fall into misunderstanding – where ego or separation is created – and understanding. There is no ultimate point of perfection. Only the truth of how it works is prefect. We can all learn more deeply about this.

Terry Rubenstein,
London,
April, 2017

Glossary and Definitions

As some terms used in this book may be unfamiliar, I have provided selected explanations below. These are intended to provide context for what has been explored in the previous pages and are not completely rigorous "dictionary" definitions. Remember also that while language is a tool we use to describe something to ourselves and each other, the whole truth always resides within, beyond the specific words and form our minds have created.

Resilience
The fact we are only ever experiencing the feeling of our thinking in the moment. This means that we are not bound by circumstances or the past. There is psychological safety, freedom, and resilience in this fact. The one obstacle that stands in the way of people being aware of their resilience is *not* recognising this fact or misunderstanding how we work psychologically.

Innate Health
Another term for resilience. The way we operate as human beings from the inside-out, which is the natural state in which all people reside. (Innate Health is often used as another term for the entire Three Principles understanding.)

The Three Principles
The three universal truths or facts that explain and account for all human psychological functioning. While these Principles cannot be separated, nor can any one of them be split from the other, they are known independently as Mind, Consciousness and Thought. It is important to know that:

Mind is not brain. It is not a thing. It is not a thought. It is the force that *acts as a catalyst* and turns Thought, whether conscious or unconscious, into the reality you now see.

Thought is not referring to your thought or my thought. It is the universal power called "Thought" which is the medium through which all of life is experienced. There are no components to Thought; it is an element that can never be broken down into smaller segments. The power of Thought, as a Principle, grants the capacity to think and creates our reality, moment to moment.

Consciousness is the medium through which our thinking is brought to life, sometimes referred to as "awareness".

Thought in the moment
There is only one place in time where we can consciously experience the power of Thought creating our experience: the present moment.

Feelings
A reaction from Thought. There is no feeling without Thought. Feelings are another word to describe moods, emotions, attitudes and states of mind.

Inside-out
The fact that our feelings are only ever coming from thought in the moment. This is constant, without exceptions.

Outside-in
Not recognising or forgetting that all feelings come from Thought in the moment. To believe that our feelings are coming from something other than Thought in the moment is an illusion and is false.

The inside-out logic of the mind/of the Three Principles paradigm
A way of referring to the immutable fact that our feelings in the moment are coming from Thought in the moment one hundred percent of the time. The unity of Thought and feeling reveals a constant logic which rules out the possibility of feelings coming from any other source.

One Discriminator
The specific and logical way of differentiating between how something works and how something does not work. Thought is a constant of our psychological experience and Thought is inseparable from the feeling of Thought. The fact of Thought as a constant brings us a single, objective and practical discriminator – that feelings are coming from Thought in the moment – can be relied upon to guide us in making sense of our experience. By establishing what is psychologically and objectively true, the inside-out rules out what is not true precisely, practically and helpfully.

Understanding
Recognising and being awake to the inside-out logic of how our mind works. This involves no "doing" and is merely an awareness of the truth of how actual reality is being created.

Misunderstanding
Failing to recognise or "forgetting" the logic of how our mind works. This occurs to all people and is not indicative of a "better" or "worse" state of mind or feeling state. We all lose sight of this logic from time to time and experience the illusion that our feelings are being caused by something other than Thought in the moment.

Implications
Any true constant will have co-occurring implications that derive from it that are logical and impersonal. In the context of this book, implications of the inside-out follow the Three Principles psychological and scientific logic of "Thought in the moment" included in all experience.

Insight
A moment of realisation when something is understood that has not been understood at that level before; sometimes referred to as "Aha" or "lightbulb" moments. Insight cannot be manufactured or worked on – it just occurs and can do so for anyone at any time.

Ego
Used in the context of this book to describe being outside-in. Thought in the moment is not included in this fallacy.

With Gratitude

I am deeply grateful to the many people – family members, friends, colleagues, students, clients, mentors and teachers – who have contributed to this book, either directly or indirectly, by being part of my ongoing journey of learning about the Three Principles. Specifically, my heartfelt thanks and appreciation go to:

Sydney Banks, without whom there would be no basis for this book and who uncovered the logic that unifies all of life and humanity.

The great many Three Principles teachers and colleagues who I am indebted to. All of you continue to inspire me to be a better student of this exquisitely deep world of truth and wisdom.

Dicken Bettinger. You have modelled for me what it is to be a person who loves and values truth so completely that it radiates from within. Your mentorship, support, wisdom, love and compassion are oxygen for the soul.

Dr Keith Blevens and Valda Monroe. Not only for the illuminating Foreword you have written, but also for your valued friendship, selfless mentorship and the rigour, patience and respect to the spiritual truth of the Principles with which you have guided me. You have been the most generous and humble of teachers in giving of your time and spirit, inviting me in to a place of learning and dialogue that has been both challenging and enlightening. Your indomitable commitment to the truth of Syd's message has touched me and so many others very deeply.

Tzvi Werther, Brett Chitty and Tess Christy. Your immense help with reviewing the manuscript and suggesting subtle but wholly significant changes is deeply appreciated. I am so grateful to all three of you for your friendship, collegiality and, most importantly, for your unapologetic rigour in service to integrity and truth.

John Scott. Your artistic talent is remarkable. Working with you was not only a delight but showcased how simply, creatively and thoughtfully the messages of these reflections can be brought to life through the medium of drawing. And of course, an enormous thank you for the inspiration behind the book's title.

Miriam Bloch. Your excellent, high-speed and highly professional editing once again made a significant difference to the final manuscript, as did your unfailing appreciation of our (not always highly professional) sense of humour!

Dan Matalon. Your outstanding cover design is spot on.

Joe Larkins and the team at Andrews UK. From our first conversation, you have aimed to make sure the job gets done fast and right, and we recognise the efforts you have gone to across the board to help get us there. And thank you Steve Emecz at MX Publishing – your generosity of spirit and belief in our work is deeply appreciated.

My Boys. Living with you all is a constant reminder that we are all created equally wise, intelligent, loving and resilient. You are my living evidence of this.

Brian. Thank you for your persistence in getting this book to and over the finish line. Your energy and vision are inspiring – though sometimes very tiring! – and while I may moan a bit (or a lot), I am forever grateful that you are gifted and tenacious enough to take my words and make them into a readable book. That is one of the many things I love and admire about you.

This book is a project of Innate Health, a non-profit organisation whose mission is sharing the understanding of innate resilience, especially to young people. At its core is a small team of incredibly hard-working, passionate and committed employees, practitioners, trustees, supporters, advisors and volunteers. I am truly inspired by each person's dedication to bringing this understanding to the world, to as many people as possible, to those who have and those who have not, to those who suffer and those who do not. It excites, humbles, challenges me and keeps me going on the days that feel tough in my mind.

I am forever grateful to the entire Innate Health team for your huge hearts, open minds, soaring spirits and for joining us on this magnificent, important and fun journey.

About the Authors

Terry Rubenstein, co-founder and Head of Education for the London-based Innate Health Centre and mother to six boys, is recognised as one of the world's leading Innate Health/Three Principles educators, practitioners and thought leaders. Since uncovering a new understanding of resilience and well-being that she never thought possible, Terry has trained under and worked with many of the pioneers in this field. Over the past twelve years, she has taught and impacted countless people in the UK and beyond, through her uplifting talks, seminars, workshops, online webinars, one-to-one sessions and extremely popular weekly Innate Health blog on which this book's reflections are based.

Terry's ground-breaking first book, the Amazom.com bestseller *Exquisite Mind – how a new paradigm transformed my life and is sweeping the world,* documents the moving account of her personal journey from mental suffering to psychological well-being and explains the Principles behind innate resilience that she has devoted her life to teaching and sharing.

Brian Rubenstein, CEO of the Innate Health Centre, has an MBA from Cass Business School, an MA in Psychotherapy and previously worked in senior roles in the City of London's financial sector as well as the non-profit educational sector. This is his fourth published book.

Terry, Brian and their six wonderful sons and King Charles Cavalier live, love and learn in North West London, where they continually reflect on and share with each other the never-ending journey of learning about the inside-out logic of the Mind.

The authors can be contacted at admin@innatehealth.co

About the Illustrator

John Scott is a coach, founder of iamJohnScott and co-creator of the unique animation, *A Curious World*. A former Creative Director, John has come to appreciate that the Three Principles understanding is not only the key to his creativity, but that it is the key for lasting, positive change in all areas of his life. His purpose as a coach is to help others see the truth in these powerful Principles of the mind for themselves. John lives in London with his wife Lizzie and their dog Loki.

He can be contacted at iamjascott@gmail.com

INNATE HEALTH

UNCOVERING RESILIENCE

Innate Health is a non-profit organisation. We offer a wide range of opportunities - individually, in group workshops and online - for you to learn about the inside-out logic of your innate resilience.

- **One to One sessions** - young people, teenagers, individuals and couples enabling this learning to be integrated into everyday life.

- **4-Day individualised 'Intensives'** - an excellent opportunity for deeper personal learning.

- **Tuesday Evening Drop-in Classes -** a range of topics and speakers.

- **Courses** - for all ages and stages: Resilience, Mums & Teens, Relationships, Further Learning and more...

- **Training Opportunities** - for present and aspiring Principle-based practitioners.

- **Website** - membership is available to access an extensive range of online learning and webinars. Go to www.innatehealth.co

---

BUILDING RESILIENCE IN THE NEXT GENERATION

IHEART

Innate Health Education
And Resilience Training

- Schools "Inside-Out Resilience" programme

- Wellbeing Bootcamps

- Innate Health Teacher Training

- Parenting Workshops

- Individual sessions for young people

For more information about any of our programmes, please contact admin@innatehealth.co
66 BRENT STREET, LONDON, NW4 2ES
020 8912 1216 Facebook: fb.com/ihclondon www.innatehealth.co
Innate Health is a non-profit organisation. Concessions available.
Registered Charity number: 1173025